KQL

A Gateway To Microsoft Sentinel

Samik Roy

ISBN-13: 978-93-100-0510-3

Cover design by: Samik Roy
Contact: samik.n.roy@gmail.com
Linkedin : https://www.linkedin.com/in/roysamik/
YouTube : https://www.youtube.com/@samikroy
Github : https://github.com/samikroy
Udemy : https://www.udemy.com/user/samik-roy-9/

CONTENTS

PREFACE

Welcome to the world of security analytics and the realm of Kusto Query Language (KQL) in Microsoft Sentinel!

As the author of this book, I am excited to go on board on this journey with us, sharing my knowledge, insights and experiences gained from navigating the intricate landscape of security operations, writing detections, workbooks which are available within Microsoft Sentinel as of today. This book is an accumulation of my passion for empowering security analysts and administrators to harness the full potential of KQL and help the explore valuable insights from their security data and stay one step ahead of evolving threats. This book will provide us an elaborated and guided path from ideation to execution of our KQL journey and will make us zero to hero in KQL.

With the rapid evolution of digital landscape, organizations face a variety of sophisticated cyber threats and security challenges. Recognizing the critical ones need effective security analysis. Microsoft Sentinel has emerged as a powerful platform which provides advanced security monitoring and intelligence capabilities. But, to harness the full potential of this platform requires a deep understanding of Kusto Query Language, the language that empowers analysts to interact with the security data. The purpose of this book is to guide us through the particulars of KQL in Microsoft Sentinel by equipping us with the knowledge and skills to uncover actionable insights and strengthen our organization's security posture.

I would like to express my deepest gratitude to the countless security professionals, analysts and administrators who have tirelessly worked to protect organizations and individuals from cyber threats. Our dedication and commitment inspire me every day. I would also like to thank the team at Microsoft and community around for their continuous innovation on the creation and evolution of Microsoft Sentinel, a groundbreaking platform that empowers security operations. Finally, I extend my appreciation to the readers of this book. Our curiosity, eagerness to learn and dedication to secure our digital world motivate me to share my expertise and experiences.

Throughout the book, we will be comprehensive about our step-by-step journey through the complexities of KQL in Microsoft Sentinel. We will start with a quick start guide, enabling us to hit the ground running with KQL and perform essential searches, projection and extension of our queries. As we progress, we will learn about advanced topics, including filtering data, leveraging joins, summarizing datasets and applying visualizations to gain deeper insights. Additionally, we will explore real-world use cases by assessing various scenarios and providing practical solutions using KQL in Microsoft Sentinel

Looking back at my years of experience in the field of security analytics, I have witnessed firsthand the transformative power of KQL in uncovering hidden threats and providing invaluable insights. Throughout this book, I aim to share not only the technical aspects of KQL but also the mindset and approach required to excel in security data analysis. My perspective is centered around the belief that security professionals can navigate the complex landscape of cyber threats and safeguard their organizations effectively by combining technical expertise with a proactive and analytical mindset.

Let's embark on this exciting journey together. I encourage us to actively engage with the chapters and take advantage of examples provided. That will allow us to apply the concepts in real-world scenarios. Embrace the challenges, experiment with different query techniques and adapt the knowledge to our unique security environment.

By the end of this book, us will have gained the skills and knowledge about writing our own queries in KQL and Microsoft Sentinel. Us will be equipped with the tools to enhance our organization's security posture, detect and respond to threats swiftly and leverage data-driven insights to drive proactive security measures.

Remember that us are part of a community of passionate

security professionals. Together, we can strengthen our collective defenses and adapt to evolving threats by protecting what matters most. I hope this book empowers us to elevate our security analysis mindset.

◆ ◆ ◆

INTRODUCTION TO KQL

Welcome to the first Chapter of this book "Introduction To KQL" where we embark on an exciting journey to master Kusto Query Language (KQL) in the context of Microsoft Sentinel. Are us ready to unlock the power of data analysis, threat detection and security operations?

In this chapter, we will introduce the basics of KQL and discover how it can be our ally in the battle against cyber threats.

Imagine ourselves as an analyst responsible for monitoring security events in our organization. We have a plethora of security logs, network data and user activity records at our disposal. But how do we make sense of this vast amount of information? How can we quickly identify patterns, detect anomalies and investigate potential security incidents? This is where KQL comes to the rescue.

KQL is a robust and versatile query language designed to efficiently query and analyze large volumes of data. It provides a rich set of features and functions that allow us to explore, filter, correlate and summarize data with ease. With KQL, we can transform raw data into actionable insights which will empower us to make informed decisions and respond quickly to potential threats.

To get a taste of KQL's power, let's consider an example. Suppose we want to analyze the failed sign-in attempts in our organization's Azure Active Directory logs. With just a few lines of KQL code, we can extract this information:

```
SigninLogs | where ResultType == "Failure" | summarize Count = count() by UserId
| order by Count desc
```

In this example, we will leverage the "SigninLogs" table, apply a filter to focus only on failed attempts and then use the "summarize" operator to count the occurrences for such users. Finally, we order the results by the count in descending order. With this query, we can identify the users experiencing the highest number of failed sign-in attempts, potentially indicating suspicious activities or credential compromise-based attacks.

When we go deeper, a typical KQL query is made up of the following:

- **A dataset** - which can be a
  - A single table.
  - Union or join of multiple tables.
  - A user defined data table.
  - Query to an external data source i.e. - a CSV or JSON file.
  - A search across all the tables.
- **A condition**- which can be one or more than one condition. An example could be.
  Where Condition on TimeGenerated
- **A projection** - This is the last section of a KQL query which if not defined projects the whole dataset.

Here is another simple example to project all the UserPrincipleName from SigninLogs for last 1 day.

SigninLogs | where TimeGenerated > ago(1d) | project UserPrincipalName
|--Dataset--|-------------Condition-------------|------------Projection---------|

All 3 components of the query are glued with a pipeline (|) operator which means output from each segment is sent as an input for the next segment.

SigninLogs ➡ where TimeGenerated > ago(1d) ➡ project UserPrincipalName

We need to follow this order to put the keywords to build an error free and logically correct query.

So, let's begin our journey into the world of KQL and discover how it can empower us to extract valuable insights, enhance our threat detection capabilities. But, before that, we get more about the details of about the toll we will using to write queries. So, let's get to know Log Analytics Explorer first.

◆ ◆ ◆

KNOW THE LOG ANALYTICS EXPLORER

Before we start learning the specific ways to write KQL and its application in Microsoft Sentinel, it is necessary to know about the Log Analytics Explorer. This powerful tool serves as a gateway to our data, enabling us to explore, visualize and interact with the vast amounts of information ingested to Microsoft Sentinel. In this sub-chapter, we will go through comprehensive overview of its features, functionalities and capabilities.

The Log Analytics Explorer is a critical component of Microsoft Sentinel that allows us to navigate and analyze the data effectively. Whether we are a security analyst, a threat hunter, or a system administrator, understanding how to leverage the Log Analytics Explorer empowers us to gain valuable insights, perform advanced queries and identify patterns or anomalies in our data. In this chapter, we lay the foundation for our journey by exploring the key aspects of the Log Analytics Explorer and guiding us through its various functionalities.

The objective of this chapter is to introduce us to the Log Analytics Explorer and equip us with the knowledge and skills to navigate and interact with our data effectively. We cover the essential features, provide step-by-step instructions on using the tool and highlight best practices for data exploration and query execution.

By the end of this chapter, we will have a solid understanding of the Log Analytics Explorer's capabilities and be ready to dive deeper into KQL in Microsoft Sentinel. So, let's get started.

We will go through various aspects of Log Analytics Explorer:

Navigating and exploring data: Log Analytics Explorer helps us to access data from various sources and explore the available data types, tables and fields.

Using the query editor: A core component of the Log Analytics Explorer is the query editor. This editor contains features like syntax highlighting, auto complete to ensure error free query creation.

We can use the **Logs** option from **Microsoft Sentinel** left navigation to access the query editor as shown in the image.

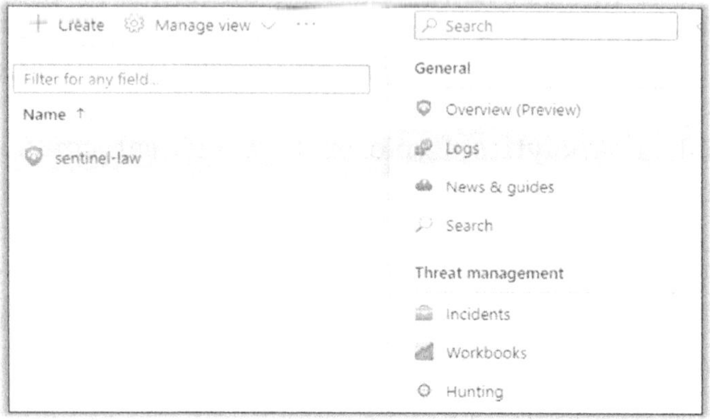

After the we arrive at the main screen of Log Analytics Explorer like the below:

The Portal is a union of 4 specific sections:

1. **Top Action Bar** :

Run Button to run the selected query in the query window. We can also use **Shift+Enter** to run a query.

Time Picker to select the time range for the data available to the query. This action is overridden if we include a time filter in the query like

```
| where TimeGenerated > ago(1d)
```

Save Button to save the current query to **Query Explorer** for the workspace either as a query or as a function.

Share Button to help us with

Copy the link to query.

Copy query text.

Copy Query Results

New Alerts Button to create one of the following:

Create Azure Monitor Alert

Create Microsoft Sentinel Alert

Export Button to Export in CSV, Excel or in the form of a PowerBI query.

Pin To button

Format Query Button

Example Query Button

Query Explorer Button

2. The left sidebar to hold the metadata tabs as

Tables – This will list down all the tables available in the Sentinel workspace.
Queries – All the Microsoft defined queries and the saved queries.
Functions – All the pre-defined functions and the ones we create in the workspace.

Filters – The option to apply filter with the left navigation.

3. The Right Query Window where we write queries with nicely built intelligence in it.

4. **The Right Bottom Result Window** shows the query history when it is opened and results when any query is executed.

To use this tool, we can use any one of the two permissions.

Microsoft Sentinel Reader

Log Analytics Reader

Visualizing data: Explore the visualization capabilities of the Log Analytics Explorer and learn how to create charts, graphs and ss

Query performance and optimization: We can leverage best practices for optimizing our queries, leveraging indexes and improving query performance within the Log Analytics Explorer.

Query structuring: Learn how to organize our queries effectively by breaking them into logical components, utilizing aliases and optimizing filter conditions.

Leveraging functions: Discover how to leverage built-in functions and create custom functions to modularize our queries, promote reusability and enhance query readability.

Query result management: Explore techniques for efficiently managing query results, including sorting, filtering and exporting data to different formats for further analysis.

Query parameterization: Understand the importance of parameterizing our queries and how it enables flexibility and scalability in our data exploration process.

Query documentation and version control: Learn the significance of documenting our queries and maintaining version control to ensure reproducibility, collaboration and auditability.

Advanced features and integrations: Get acquainted with advanced features and integrations available within the Log Analytics Explorer, such as saved searches, alerts and data export options.

The Log Analytics Explorer is a foundational tool in Microsoft Sentinel that enables us to interact with our data and unleash its full potential. By knowing Log Analytics Explorer in depth, we gain the ability to navigate and explore our data efficiently, perform advanced queries and uncover valuable insights. This chapter serves as a steppingstone, setting the stage for our journey into KQL for Microsoft Sentinel, where we will further leverage the Log Analytics Explorer's capabilities to conduct robust security analysis and drive actionable outcomes.

◆ ◆ ◆

QUICK START OUR KQL WITH SENTINEL

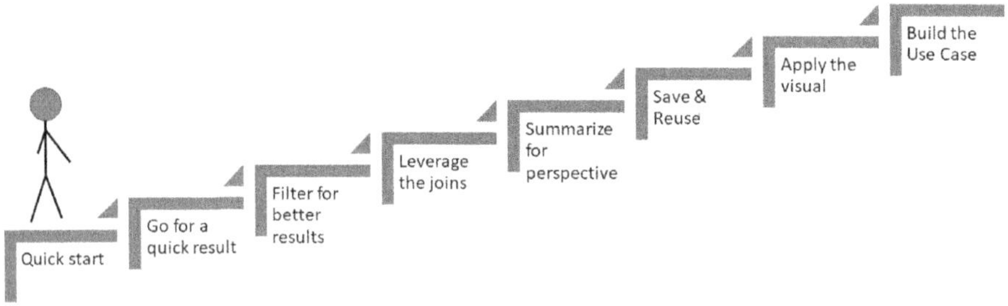

◆ ◆ ◆

After we have seen the Log Analytics Interface, it is time to get stated with writing our first KQL query. And in this chapter, "Quick Start our KQL with Sentinel", we get started on an exciting journey to write our first query and start on the journey to be ally in the battle against cyber threats.

The objective of this chapter to provide us the ability to extract actionable insights from vast amount of data becomes crucial. So, we will get equipped with the process to write our very first query to get started with information extraction using KQL. We will explore key techniques and best practices to streamline our searches, project relevant data and extend our query capabilities on the fly.

In this chapter, we will explore on starting our KQL with **Search** by introducing the basic structure of a KQL query and the importance of the 'Search' operator.

Projecting the required columns to narrow down our query results by selecting specific columns and discarding unnecessary data.

Extending the query to build columns on the fly and discover how to dynamically create new columns within our query to enhance data analysis and gain deeper insights.

By the end of this chapter, we will have a solid foundation to build our queries from scratch and start extracting the results. So, let's get started.

◆ ◆ ◆

Start our KQL with Search

The very first KQL query should start with a search. Once we have opened the Logs blade in Microsoft Sentinel, we can start our query with a search command. The reason here is, it is one of its kind of command which lets us query the entire workspace. And the ways us can leverage search are:

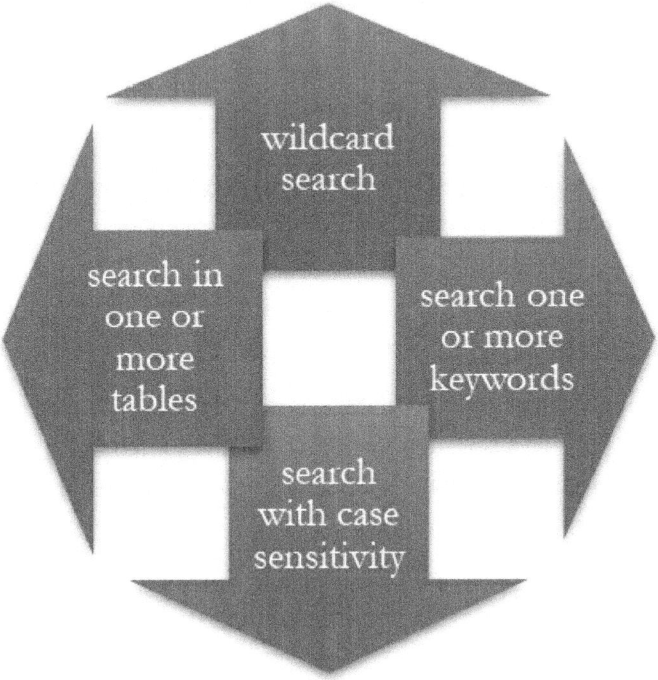

Here are ways we can use wildcard search:

➢ **First**, we can write our first search query to search a particular keyword.
For example, if we want to search across all the data sources, we can use the following query:

search "OfficeActivity"

This query retrieves all data sources with all the columns where "OfficeActivity" word is found.

Here are ways we can use to search one or more keywords:

➢ **Next**, we can apply search in a conditional way with multiple keywords, to search matching terms.

For example, if we want to search for "admin" and either "office" or "azure" we can use the following query.

search "admin" and ("office" or "azure")

This query retrieves all data sources with all the columns where the combination of "**admin**" and "**office**" otherwise "**admin**" and "**azure**" word are found.

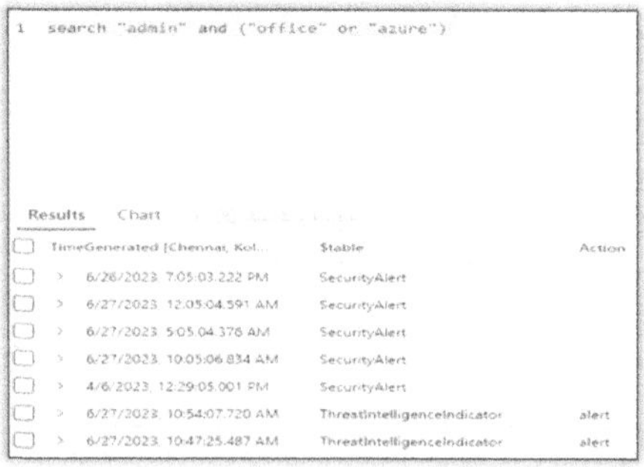

Here are ways we can use case sensitive searches:

➢ **Next**, we can search with case sensitive words to match an exact case.

For example, if we want to search for the admin keyword inside SigninLogs, we can use the following query:

search kind=case_sensitive "Admin" and ("SigninLogs" or OfficeActivity")

search kind=case_sensitive "admin" and ("SigninLogs" or "OfficeActivity")

This query will display the rows from SigninLogs or OfficeActivity table where any of the columns contains "Admin" or "admin" respectively.

Here are ways we can use search within specific tables:

Next, we can search for a particular keyword within a table.

For example, if we want to search for the admin keyword inside SigninLogs , we can use the following query

search in (SigninLogs) "admin"

This query will display the rows from SigninLogs table where any of the columns contains "**admin**".

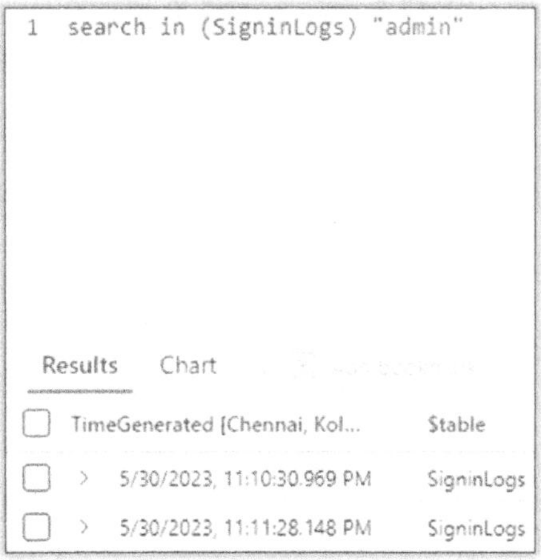

Next, we can search in multiple tables.

For example, if we want to search for the "**admin**" or "**azure**" keyword across all the tables start with Signin or tables named OfficeActivity then we can use the following query:

search in (Signin*, OfficeActivity) "admin" or "azure"

This query will display the rows from all the tables starts with Signin or OfficeActivity table where any of the columns contains "**admin**" or "**azure**"

Next, we can search over on a combined dataset.
For example, if we want to search for the "Azure" or " ubuntuvm " or "Office" across all the tables starting with Signin and Heartbeat table then we can use the following query :

union Signin*, Heartbeat | search "Azure" or "ubuntuvm" or "Office"

This query will display the rows from all the tables starts with Signin or Heartbeat table where any of the columns contains "**Azure**" or " **ubuntuvm** " or "**Office**"

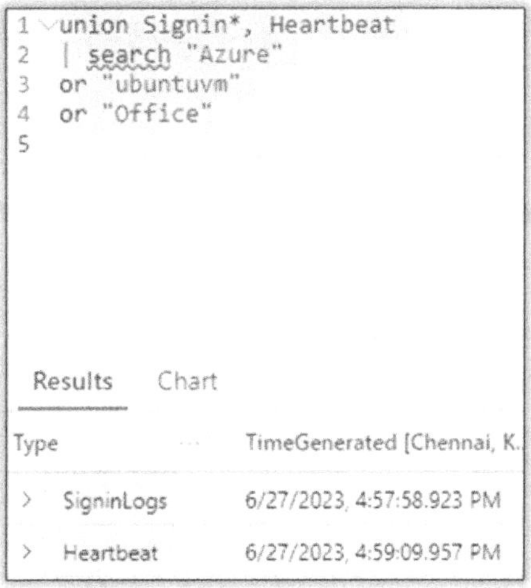

Please scan the qr below for a demo

*In summary "**search**" can be used in various ways:*

- ✓ *We can search across all the data sources.*
- ✓ *We can apply search conditionally.*
- ✓ *Add case sensitivity to our search.*
- ✓ *Search one more than one keyword in a single table or across multiple tables. Search on a combined data set, like a local dataset and an external dataset.*

Now it is time for us to create our own search query either by using one or more methods mentioned above.

◆ ◆ ◆

Project the required columns

◆ ◆ ◆

After receiving the search results with plenty of columns there might be information overload. Now to ease it we use Project to display only specific columns.

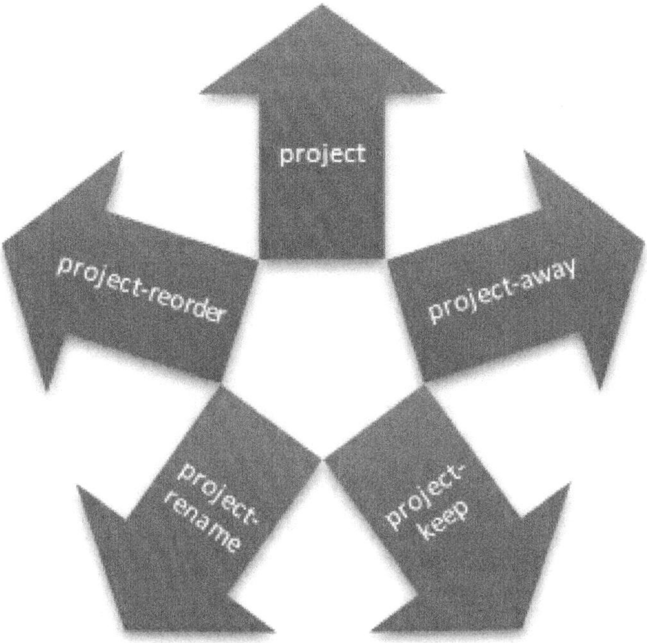

We can use project with several ways based on our need for the columns to be displayed.

➢ **First**, we can project a single column from the dataset.
For example, if we want to display only UserPrincipalName from SigninLogs then we can use the following query: ***SigninLogs | project UserPrincipalName***

This query displays only UserPrincipalName from SigninLogs.

We can exclude certain columns if we feel that the data inside the column is redundant.
For example, if we want to exclude OperationName column from the results of SigninLogs then we can use the following query:

SigninLogs | project-away OperationName

This query will list all the columns excluding OperationName column from SigninLogs table.
Another example can be excluding more than column starting with a common phase.
Let's say we want to exclude some of any column which starts with Operation then we can use the below query:

SigninLogs | project-away Operation*

This query will exclude all the columns starting with Operation from SigninLogs table.
We can introduce a new column using project statement.
For example, if we want to create a new column on the fly from the results of SigninLogs then we can use the following query:

SigninLogs | project UserPrinipalName, NewColumn = strcat('User - ', UserPrinipalName)

This query will generate new column as a part of the result set.

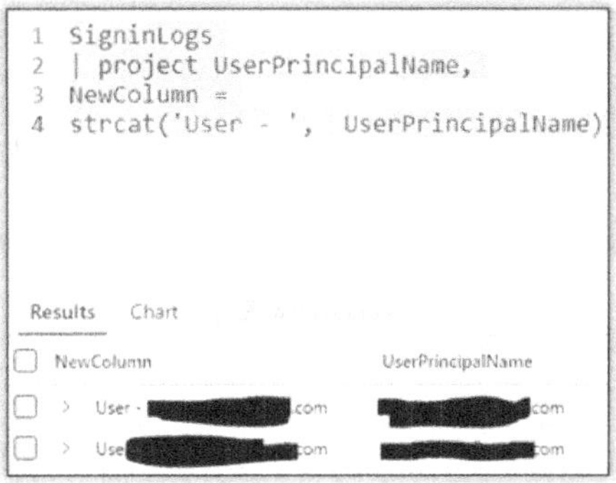

➢**Next**, there will be cases where we would like to keep only a few columns.
For example, if we want to keep only a few columns then we can use the following query:

SigninLogs | project-keep OperationName

This query will display only the column named OperationName.

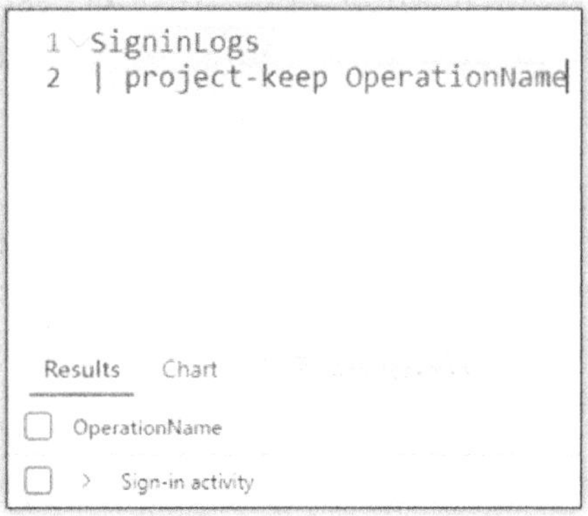

➢**Next**, there will be cases where we would like to keep only a few columns, like above by with a bit of wild card for the column with similar names.
For example, if we want to keep only columns starting with Operation, then we can use the following query.

SigninLogs | project-keep Operation*

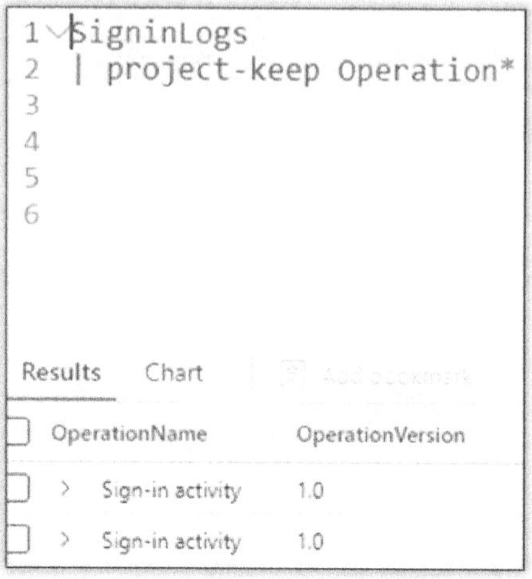

This query will display only the column with a specific set of columns to have operation as a key word.

➢**Next**, after we have removed the unnecessary columns with project-away or we have only kept the necessary column with project-keep, we will still find some more columns which are needed but do not have a good column name attached.

We can rename them. For example, we want to provide a UserPrincipalName as a NewColumn , we can use the below query:

SigninLogs | project-rename NewColumn = UserPrincipalName

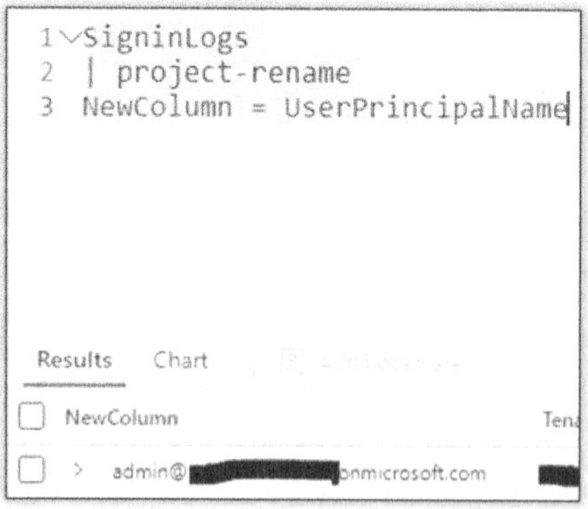

As a result, the result it will rename the column as UserPrincipalName as NewColumn when the result sets are displayed.

➢**Next**, while we write a project statement we might not get the result in the correct sequence, so we can use project-reorder to reorder the list of displayed columns.For example, we can use the below query to display the UserPrincipalName at first and display the result of the
columns.

SigninLogs | project-reorder

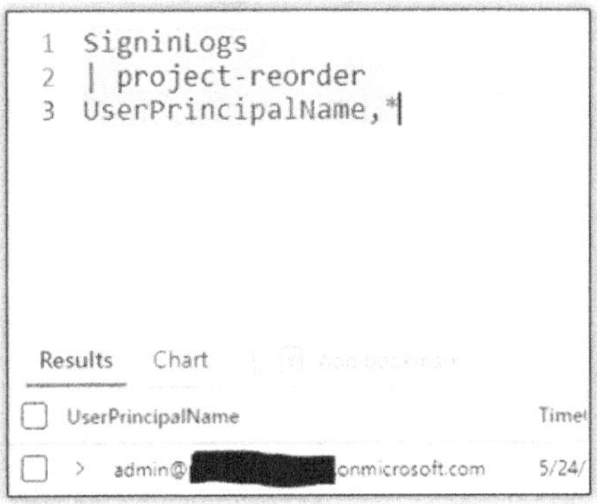

As a result the result it will display the UserPrincipalName as a the first column and then will display the rest of the column without repeating the UserPrincipalName again.

➢**We** can go a step further with this if we want to display the similar type of columns at the beginning and then the rest. For example, we can use the below query:

SigninLogs | project-reorder User*,*

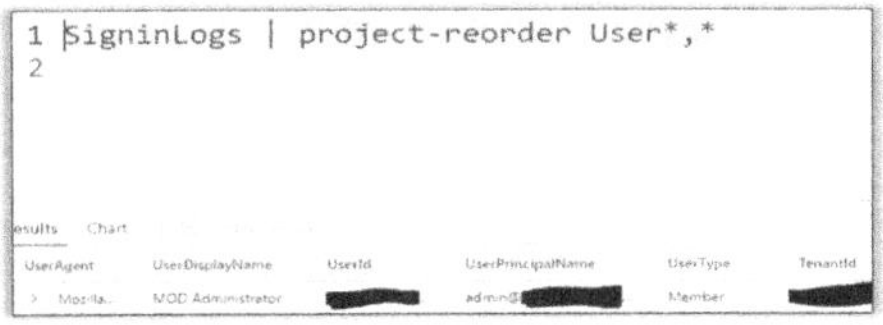

This will display the results with the columns starting with User and then the rest of the columns.

Please scan the qr below for a demo

In summary, project is a multi-facet statement. We use them on the occasions of

- ✓ *selection of one or more columns*
- ✓ *hiding one more column*
- ✓ *structure our output like which column should appear in what sequence.*

So, we can use the combination of one or more methods mentioned above to prepare our project statement.

◆ ◆ ◆

Extend the query to build the columns on the fly

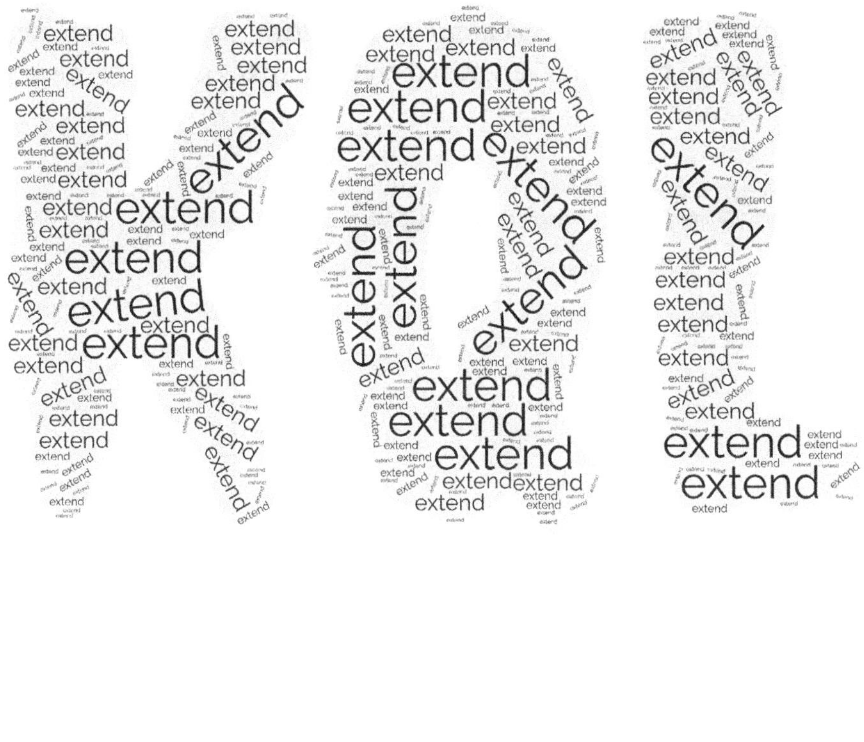

Now when we search for a particular information with KQL and find that, but that data is somehow available inside any complex structure like an array, a long message etc. Or we might need to perform some calculations with existing and display in a new column then extend operator helps us here.

- Extend Multiple Columns
- Extend Multiple Times

➢**First**, we want to calculate some value in terms of the existing data.

For example, if we want to calculate how long back an event was generated from the TimeGenerated column in SigninLogs then we can use the following query:

SigninLogs
| summarize max(TimeGenerated)
| extend LoggedOffSinceMinutes = datetime_diff('minute',now(),max_TimeGenerated)

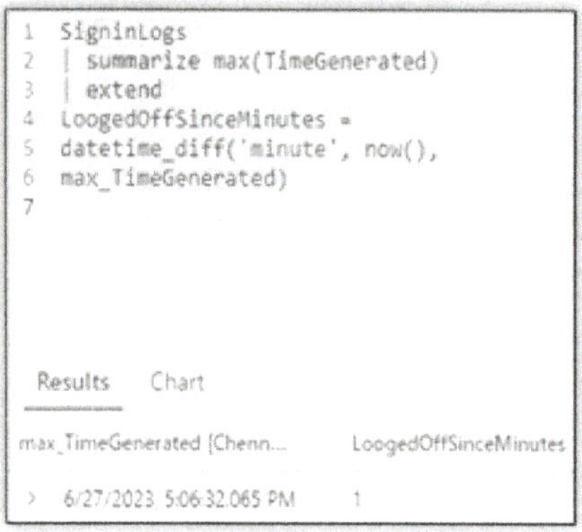

This query displays 2 columns as output TimeGenerated, LoogedOffSinceMinutes.

➢**We** can have multiple extend commands and use the previous column as a reference to the next.

For example, in addition to the previous query we also want to see the output in days then we can use the below query

SigninLogs | summarize max(TimeGenerated)
|extend LoggedOffSinceMinutes = datetime_diff('minute',now(),max_TimeGenerated)
| extend LoggedOffSinceDay = LoggedOffSinceMinutes/60/24

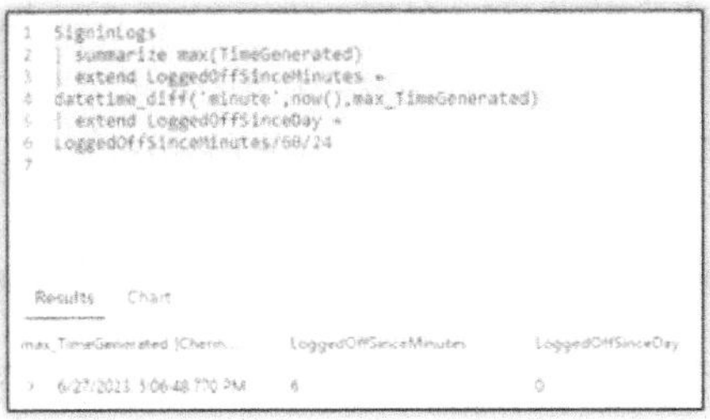

This query displays 3 columns as output TimeGenerated, LoogedOffSinceMinutes, LoogedOffSinceDay

We will need to use extend in our queries every now and then. The only point to keep in mind that if we want use extend to create new columns and display them, we can do that with the same extend statement. But, if we want to use any column generated by extend to be used in the query further, we must use multiple extend statements, like the below:

SigninLogs | summarize max(TimeGenerated)

⬇

| extend LoggedOffSinceMinutes =

⬇

datetime_diff('minute',now(),max_TimeGenerated)

⬇

| extend LoggedOffSinceDay = LoggedOffSinceMinutes/60/24

Please scan the qr below for a demo

In Summary, extend helps us create columns on the fly. So, whenever we are using extend, we need to keep in mind about using:

✓ *Projecting all the columns which are needed to be used in extend.*

✓ *Remove the unnecessary columns.*

◆ ◆ ◆

GO FOR A QUICK RESULT

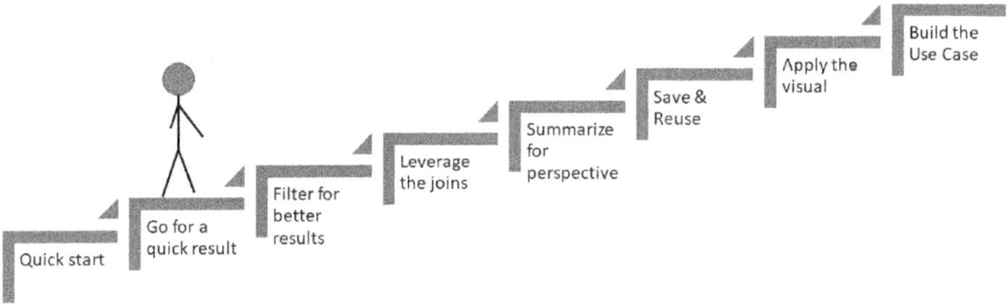

◆ ◆ ◆

After writing the first KQL query, it is also important that we learn a way to get quick results. And in this chapter, "Go for a quick result", we will explore techniques to obtain quick and concise results from our data queries using two primary ways, the "count" operator and the "distinct" operator.

The objective of this chapter is to help extract quick results from our query in Microsoft Sentinel. By exploring the results, we will gain an understanding of data distribution & uniqueness of the dataset. By mastering idea of quick results, we will be able to expedite our data analysis process and derive meaningful insights swiftly or tune our query at faster pace.

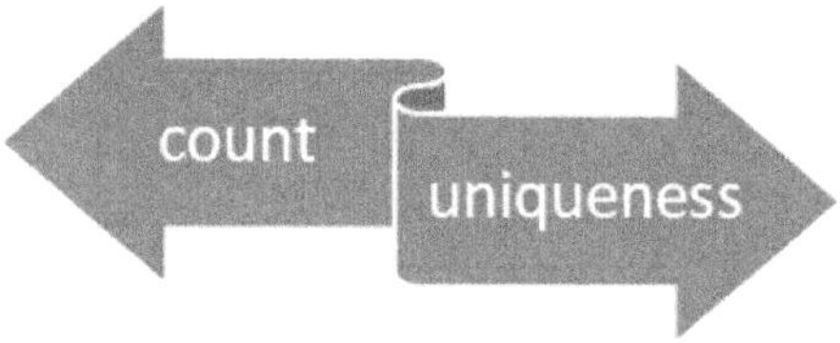

Throughout this chapter, we will experience practical examples to solidify our understanding of the "count" and "distinct" operators. We will explore real-world scenarios where these techniques are invaluable for time-sensitive investigations and threat analysis.

The "count" operator allows us to obtain a quick output by counting the number of records that match specific criteria. We will go through examples where we can leverage this operator to get an immediate overview of events or to track the occurrence of specific activities or anomalies. We will learn how to apply filters and aggregation functions in conjunction with "count" to tailor our results and focus on the most critical insights.

Next, the "distinct" operator, which helps identify unique values within a specific field or column. This operator is particularly useful when we want to find distinct entities, such as unique IP addresses, user accounts or event types. By using "distinct," we can quickly identify patterns, detect outliers and gain a deeper understanding of our data's uniqueness.

By the end of this this chapter, we will be able to obtain quick and concise results which will empower us to understand the direction of writing query, tweak the query further to make the results more precise as per the need. So, let's get started with this chapter and know more about the outcomes we can get from of a quick result.

◆ ◆ ◆

Use count for a quick output

◆◆◆

Getting a count is an important part of a query where we realize is if our query is giving expected number of results.

➢ First, we want to find the count for any given query.

For example, if we want to find the count for SigninLogs table then we can use the below query:

SigninLogs | count

This query will just provide us the count from SigninLogs table.

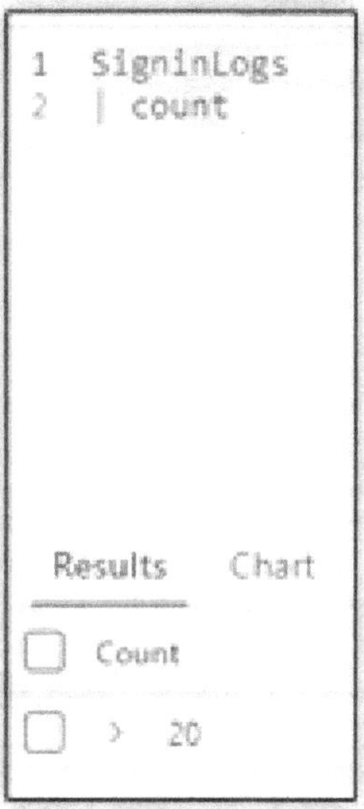

➢ Then, if we want to find the count of certain distinct values.

For example, if we want to find the count for each UserPrincipalName in SigninLogs table then we can use the below query

SigninLogs | summarize count() by UserPrincipalName

This query will provide the count for each UserPrincipalName from SigninLogs table. Count is used as a function in this case.

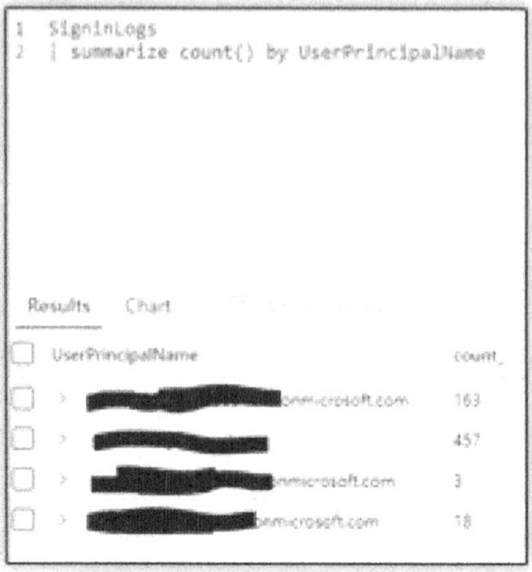

Please scan the qr below for a demo

In summary, count is a no brainer, it provides us number as an essence and provides an estimate of the query we are writing. This is very helpful when we are writing a query and it might return several results. Well, count will give a quick glace through the numbers to help us decide if we are on the right track.

◆ ◆ ◆

Use distinct for to find unique values

While we write a query getting distinct vales are a clear proof of our hypothesis. Now, there are a few ways how distinct operator can help here

➢ First, we want to find distinct values for a single column in a table or dataset.

For example, if we want to find the UserPrincipalName from SigninLogs then we can use the below query:

SigninLogs| distinct UserPrincipalName

This query will list all the unique list of UserPrincipalName from SigninLogs

➢ We want a unique value for combination of columns.

For example, if we want to find the unique combination of AppDisplayName & UserPrincipalName from SigninLogs then we can use the below query:

SigninLogs | distinct UserPrincipalName, AppDisplayName

This query will list all the unique set of rows for a combination of UserPrincipalName & AppDisplayName.

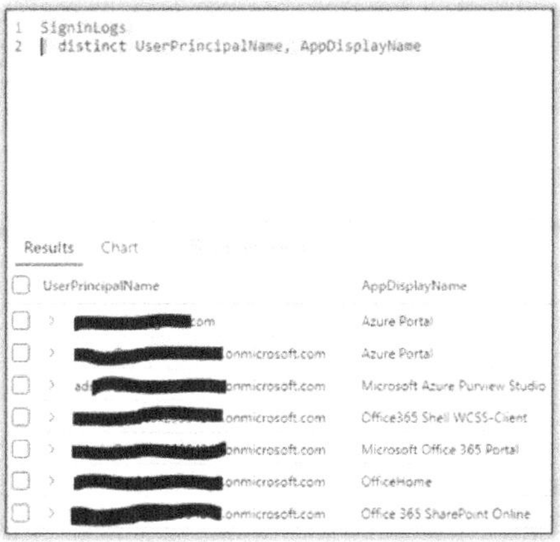

➢ We want to find distinct values across datasets

For example, if we want find the unique UserPrincipalName from SigninLogs & AADNonInteractiveUserSignInLogs then we can use the query:

union SigninLogs, AADNonInteractiveUserSignInLogs

| distinct UserPrincipalName,Type

This query will list all the unique UserPrincipalName from SigninLogs & AADNonInteractiveUserSignInLog

➢ Another one is, if we want to find the unique set of rows for a combination of UserPrincipalName & AppDisplayName from SigninLogs & AADNonInteractiveUserSignInLogs then us can use the below query

union SigninLogs, AADNonInteractiveUserSignInLogs

| distinct UserPrincipalName, AppDisplayName

This query will list all the unique set of rows for a combination of UserPrincipalName & AppDisplayName from SigninLogs & AADNonInteractiveUserSignInLog

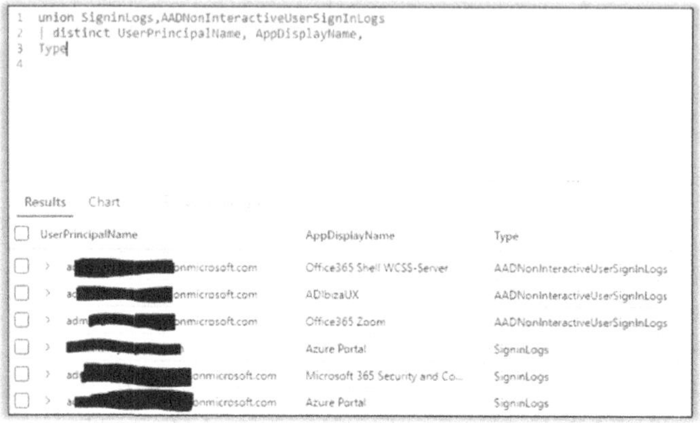

Please scan the qr below for a demo

Like count, distinct provides us a detail of values out of our query. So, when we are writing the query running distinct is very powerful option to know the unique values of our result set. It will help to structure our query in a better way.

◆ ◆ ◆

FILTER FOR BETTER RESULTS

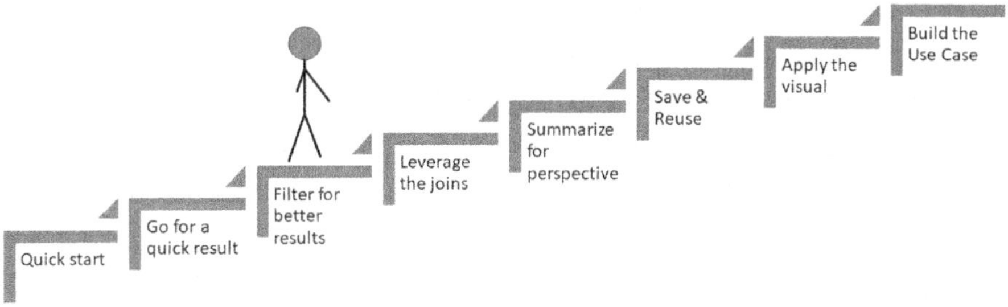

◆◆◆

Building on the knowledge gained in the previous chapters, where we explored the foundations of KQL queries and techniques for obtaining quick results, we now turn our attention to the importance of filtering data to improve the quality and relevance of our analysis.

The objective of this chapter is to introduce us to the art of filtering in KQL, fundamental skill in data analysis and plays a vital in security operations. In the vast sea of security data, finding the relevant information can be like searching for a needle in a haystack as not all data points are created equal and traversing through large volumes of data can be time-consuming and overwhelming. But fear not! In this chapter, "Filter for Better Results", we will equip with the with the details to navigate through the data flood using KQL.

Throughout this chapter, we will traverse through the process of applying where conditions in our queries to filter data effectively in conjunction with AND / OR condition to construct complex filtering conditions and utilizing comparison operators (equal to, not equal to, greater than, less than, etc.) to specify precise filtering criteria. In addition, exploring string operators and functions for text-based filtering. Furthermore, we will leverage time-based filtering to narrow down our data set to specific time ranges or intervals.

By the end of this chapter, we will have a better understanding of how to harness the filtering capabilities of KQL to streamline our data analysis and discover critical security insights. So, let's get started with this chapter and know more about the possibility of a getting better results with the right filters allowing us to narrow our focus and uncover timely insights.

◆ ◆ ◆

Apply where condition to filter better

◆ ◆ ◆

Once we have figured out the base query and our hypothesis is proved with the results we have received. Now it is time to apply where condition to increase the accuracy & efficiency of the query.

➢ First, we filter our query results only for a certain period.

For example, if we want filter our query results for last 1 day then we can use the below query:

SigninLogs | where TimeGenerated >ago(1d)

This query will list all the results given within last 24hours or 1 day from SigninLogs.

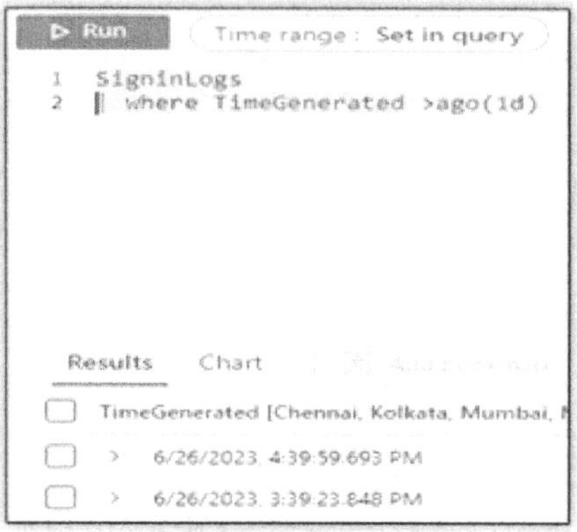

➢ Next, if we want to apply the filter on a bracket

For example, we want to filter between last 1 day and last 12 hours we can use the below query

SigninLogs | where TimeGeneated > ago(1d) and TimeGenerated <(12h)

And this query will return the result between last 1 day and last 12 hours.

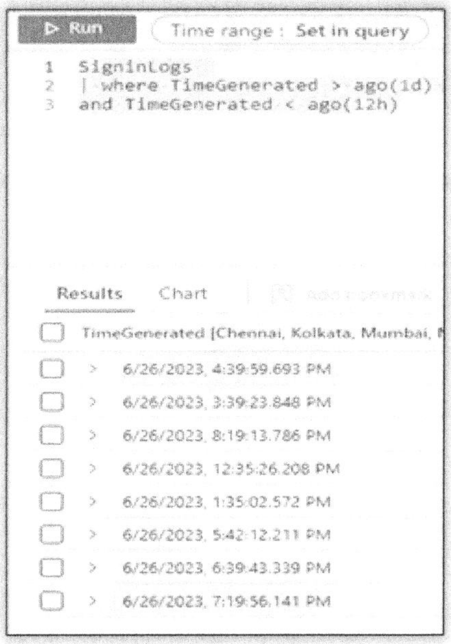

➢ If we want to apply filter on a particular column.

For example, if we want apply filter on UserPrincipalName in SigninLogs then we can use the below query:

SigninLogs | where UserPrincipalName contains "admin"

This query will list all the results by filtering UserPrincipalName column with the provide value from SigninLogs.

➢ Next, we can combine where conditions for a better filter.

For example, we want to get SigninLogs for last 1day and for a specific UserPrincipalName, we can use the below query

SigninLogs | where TimeGenerate > ago(1d) and UserPrincipalName contains "admin"

This will result where both the conditions are matched.

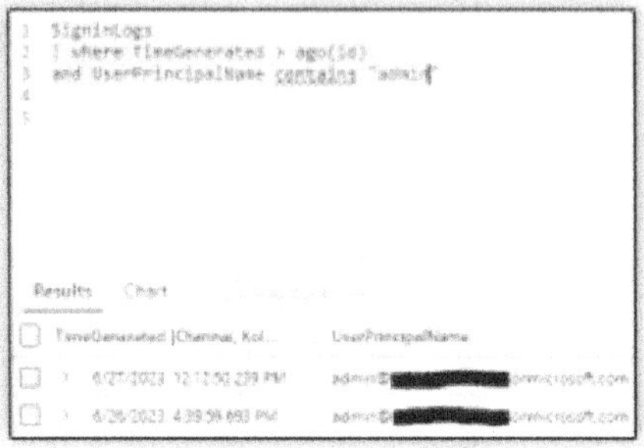

➢ To go a bit deeper, we can have multiple where conditions and apply them in a sequence to have an optimized query.
For example, we have a where for last 1 day and then based on the data from 1 day can apply another filter on UserPrincipalName and we can use the below query to achieve the same.

SigninLogs | where TimeGenerated > ago(1d)
| where UserPrincipalName contains "admin"

This will result where both the conditions are matched

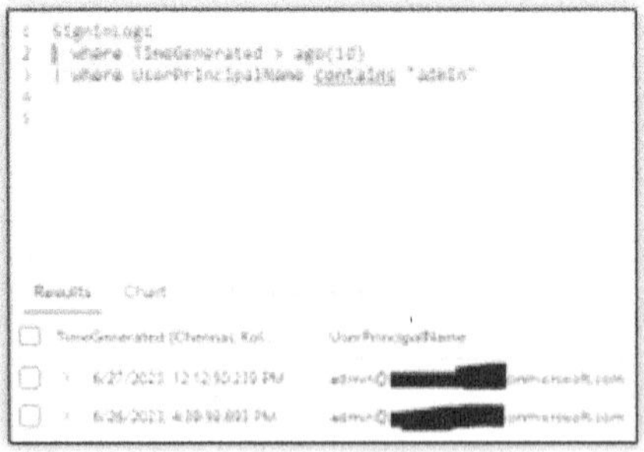

➢ Next, to apply the filter to a bigger scope, let's say, we want to filter across multiple data sources.
For example, we want to search for a GUID across SigninLogs and OfficeActivity, we can use the below query

union SigninLogs,OfficeActivity | where * has "admin"

It will display the results from both the tables.

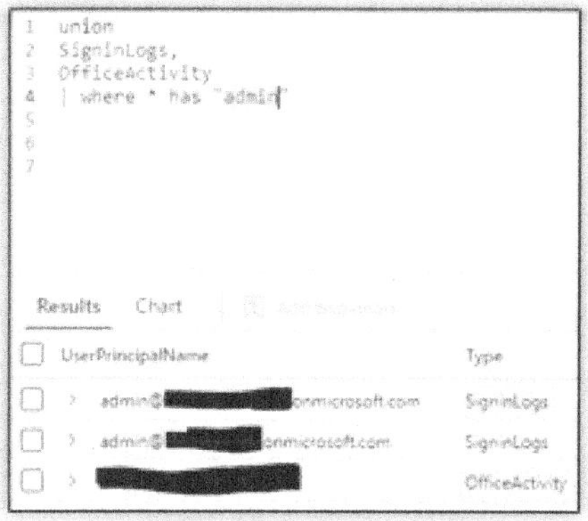

Please scan the qr below for a demo

Now, to draw a bottom line where condition can be used:
On a particular dataset
Multiple time on the same dataset (with or without a pipeline)
Perform a search.

◆ ◆ ◆

Filter our data set with time generated

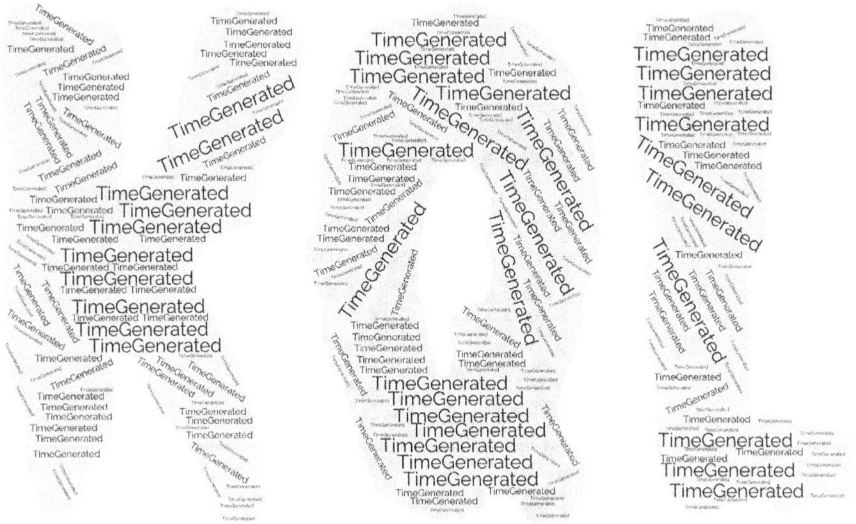

Before we start with TimeGenerated, there is unique thing about TimeGenerated column in Log Analytics / Microsoft Sentinel.

This is a common column available in every dataset / table created.

Each row can be separated with TimeGenerated field.

Our query becomes more accurate when we know within what Time frame we are looking for the results.

So, apply a filter on timestamp is one of the best filters to have.

➢ First, we want to apply a single time filter:

For example, if we want to filter our query results for last 24 hours then we can use the below query

SigninLogs | where TimeGenerated >ago(24h)

This query will list all the results given within last 24hours from SigninLogs.

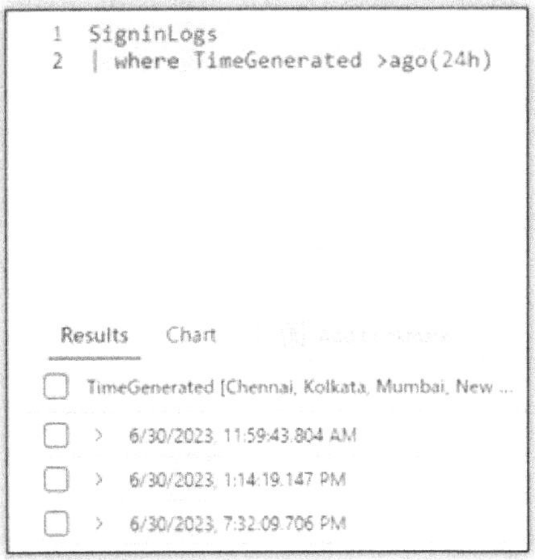

If we want to apply a time filter within bracket of time.

For example, if we want to view a data for last 3 excluding the last day then we can use the below query

SigninLogs | where TimeGenerated > ago(3d) and TimeGenerated < ago(1d)

This query will list all the results given within last 3 days except for the last 24 hours from SigninLogs.

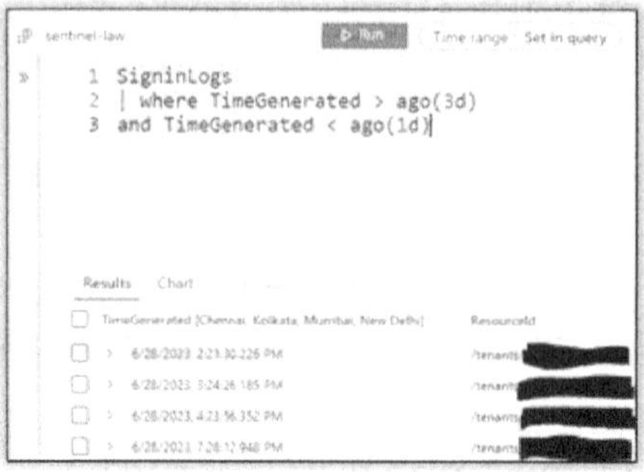

➢ If we want to get the data from the beginning of the day. For example, if we want to view a data for last 3 excluding the last day but from start of the day till end of the day then we can use the below query:

SigninLog | where TimeGenerated > startofday(ago(3d))

and TimeGenerated < startofday(ago(1d))

This query will list all the results from given within last 3 days from the start of the day except for the last 1 days start of the day from SigninLogs.

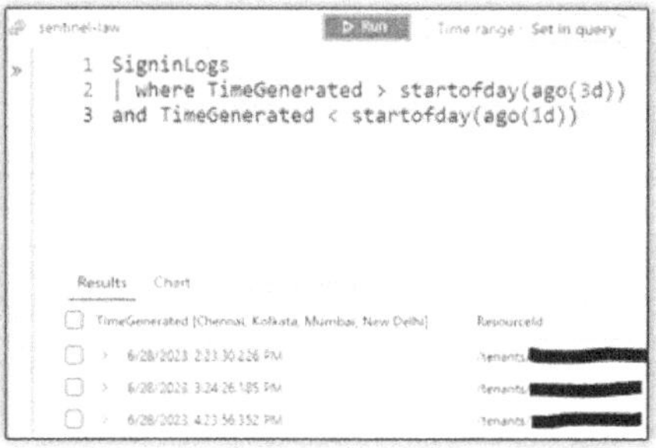

➢ If we want to get the data from between an exact time frame. For example, if we want to view a data from a particular time from last 3 to a particular time frame excluding the last day but from start of the day till end of the day then we can use the below query

SigninLogs

| where TimeGenerated between (datetime (2022-12-13) .. datetime (2022-12-16, 20:00))

This query will list all the results from a particular time from last 3 to a particular time frame excluding the last from SigninLogs.

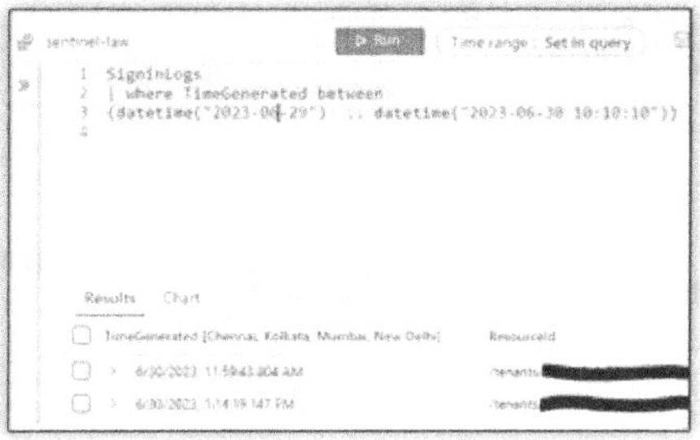

The same bracket can be applied in terms of time unit like minutes, hours & days.

SigninLogs | where TimeGenerated between

(startofday(ago(48h)) .. endofday(ago(1d)))

Please scan the qr below for a demo

In Summary, we can apply filter on TimeGenerated column in various ways to bracket the results:

✓ *Using a specific time with ago().*

✓ *Using a start time and end time*

✓ *Using start of the day and end of the days or even any specific time of the day*

✓ *Remember, TimeGenerated is always on UTC and so as the filters.*

◆ ◆ ◆

Parse the right way

Parsing in KQL is the process of extracting relevant information from raw data to gain insights and perform meaningful analysis. It allows us to break down complex data structures and extract specific components. For example, consider a log entry containing various fields such as timestamp, source IP, destination IP and event type. By using parse operations, we can extract each field separately and analyze the data based on specific attributes.

Though out, we will be using thew below example documented by Microsoft to analyze files based on their properties or organize them in a structured manner.

```
let Table_Raw_Log_Data = datatable(CustomEventText: string)
[
 "CustomEvent: InfoEvent (resourceName=CustomApplication, totalSlices=27, sliceNumber=23, lockTime=02/17/2016 08:40:01, releaseTime=02/17/2016 08:40:01, previousLockTime=02/17/2016 08:39:01)",
 "CustomEvent: WarningEvent (resourceName=CustomApplication, totalSlices=27, sliceNumber=15, lockTime=02/17/2016 08:40:00, releaseTime=02/17/2016 08:40:00, previousLockTime=02/17/2016 08:39:00)",
 "CustomEvent: ExceptionEvent (resourceName=CustomApplication, totalSlices=27, sliceNumber=20, lockTime=02/17/2016 08:40:01, releaseTime=02/17/2016 08:40:01, previousLockTime=02/17/2016 08:39:01)"
];
```

Let's look at the different parsing options available:

Parsing with Delimiters: Delimiter-based parsing allows us to extract meaningful data by splitting strings into multiple parts using separators or delimiters. Let's consider the data set mentioned above that includes a message with various fields separated by commas. By employing parse operations with the delimiter as a comma, we can extract each field individually and gain insights from specific attributes such as resourceName, totalSlices, sliceNumber etc.

```
Table_Raw_Log_Data
| parse CustomEventText with * "resourceName=" resourceName ", totalSlices=" totalSlices: long * "sliceNumber=" sliceNumber: long * "lockTime=" lockTime ", releaseTime=" releaseTime: date "," * "previousLockTime=" previousLockTime: date ")" *
| project resourceName, totalSlices, sliceNumber, lockTime, releaseTime, previousLockTime
```

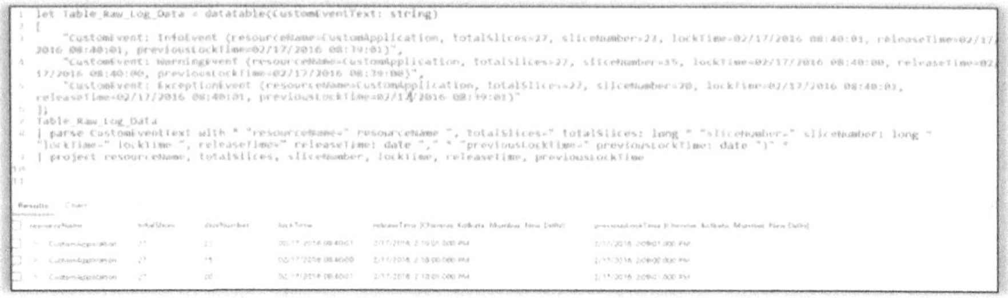

Parsing with Regular Expressions: Regular expressions provide advanced parsing capabilities in KQL, enabling us to define custom patterns and extract complex data structures. Let's consider the data set mentioned above that includes a message with various fields separated by commas. By using a regular expression, we can extract the resourceName, totalSlices from the CustomEventText, allowing us to analyze and identify patterns in the data.

```
Table_Raw_Log_Data
| parse kind = regex CustomEventText with "(.*?)[a-zA-Z]*=" resourceName @", totalSlices=\s*\d+\s*.*?
sliceNumber=" sliceNumber: long  ".*?(previous)?lockTime=" lockTime ".*?releaseTime=" releaseTime
".*?previousLockTime=" previousLockTime: date "\\)"
 | project resourceName, sliceNumber, lockTime, releaseTime, previousLockTime
```

Parsing Timestamps and Dates: Parsing timestamps and dates in KQL is essential for analyzing time-based data. Suppose we have a timestamp field representing the creation time of events. By applying parse operations, we can extract the year, month and day from the timestamp. This enables us to analyze trends, identify patterns over time, or group data based on specific time intervals.

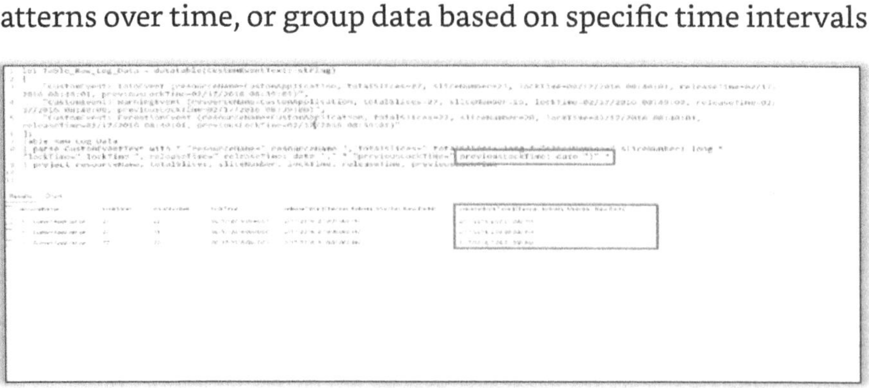

Parsing JSON Data: JSON parsing in KQL allows us to extract relevant information from structured JSON data. Let's say, we have a JSON payload containing information about user login. By using **parse_json**, we can extract specific attributes such as Login Details and Success which might enable us to perform further analysis:

```
let User_Login='{"UserName":"admin_user", "Login_Detaiils":"{\\"Success\\":true, \\"HybridUser\
\":true}"}';
print User_Login_Status=
  parse_json(tostring(parse_json(User_Login).Login_Detaiils)).Success
```

Parsing XML Data: KQL provides the capability to parse XML data and extract desired elements or attributes. Let's use the same example as above with **parse_xml**

```
let User_Login =
"<?xml version=\"1.0\" encoding=\"UTF-8\"?><UserName>admin</
UserName><Login_Details><Success>true</Success><HybridUser>true</HybridUser></
Login_Details>";
  print User_Login_Status = parse_xml(User_Login).Login_Details.Success
```

To summarize, parse operation can be utilized make the unstructured data to a structured and readable format. As a result, the output becomes more readable which helps to assess the data at a faster pace. In the process, we should follow the best practice to improve query performance and they are:

- *Choose the right parse operation that are suitable for the data structure. We can use one or more parsing techniques to write our queries.*
- *Choose the right datatype while parsing.*
- *Avoid parsing additional columns which are not necessary.*
- *Apply error handling with isnull() function to check for null values.*
- *Additionally, start writing the parsing query with a minimal amount of data like by using take 1.*

A good place to utilize parsing is on network traffic logs, logs from

Syslog based appliances.

◆ ◆ ◆

LEVERAGE THE JOINS

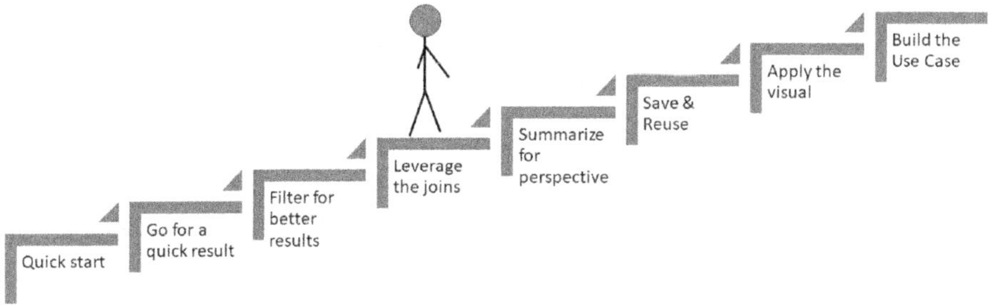

◆◆◆

Leveraging the joins across dataset is one of the best possible ways to correlate the data. Data massaging helps to get better visibility. By leveraging joins, we can uncover valuable insights and perform complex data analysis tasks.

The objective of this chapter is to get a deeper understanding into the world of joins in KQL and explore various techniques to effectively combine and correlate data from different tables. We will focus on the fundamental concepts and advanced techniques that will enable us to harness the full potential of joins in our data analysis workflow.

In the following sections, we will explore different types of joins, including inner joins, left anti joins, left outer joins and cross joins. We will discuss their unique characteristics, use cases and provide examples to illustrate how to leverage these join operations effectively.

Additionally, we will dig deeper into advanced join techniques such as subqueries, joining on multiple columns and applying join conditions. These techniques allow us to perform more complex data analysis tasks, filter joined data and tailor our queries to extract the most relevant information.

Throughout this chapter, we will gain the knowledge and understanding required to navigate the world of joins in KQL confidently. By the end, us will be able to and unleash the full potential of our data analysis capabilities in Azure Data Explorer.

By the end of this chapter, we will gain the ability to extract deeper insights, identify relationships and make informed decisions based on comprehensive data analysis by combining data from multiple tables seamlessly to bridge the gap between disparate data sources, enabling us to uncover hidden patterns and correlations that may not be apparent when working with individual tables alone. So, let's get started with this chapter and know more about the various ways of using joins in our query.

◆ ◆ ◆

Correlate multiple datasets with joins

Joins in KQL are like any other language and we will be using a specific set example to understand the concepts of joins in KQL and corelate them with one another.

Here are the sample dataset.

```
let Left_Data_Table = datatable(LeftKey:string, Continent:string)
['key1','South America', 'key2','Europe','key2','Australia', 'key3','North America'];

let Right_Data_Table = datatable(RightKey:string, Country:string)
 ['key2','France','key3','Canada','key3','Greenland','key4','India'];
```

The dataset will look like the below when projected as table in KQL.

Left_Data_Table		**Right_Data_Table**	
LeftKey	*Country*	*RightKey*	*Continent*
Key 1	*South America*	*Key 2*	*France*
Key 2	*Europe*	*Key 3*	*Canada*
Key 2	*Australia*	*Key 3*	*Greenland*
Key 3	*North America*	*Key 4*	*India*

Each type of join has 4 components:

Dataset on the left-hand side which can contain a table or a set of tables, basically a dataset.

Dataset on the right-hand side which can contain a table or a set of tables, basically another dataset.

The Join kind, through which both the data sets will be connected.

The on condition, based on which the matches will be made. There can be one or more columns which can be matched.

- The first kind of join is **innerunique**, here is the query for the above-mentioned data tables.

```
Left_Data_Table
```

```
| join kind=innerunique Right_Data_Table
  on $left.LeftKey == $right.RightKey
```

As a result

Left_Data_Table		***Right_Data_Table***	
LeftKey	*Continent*	*RightKey*	*Continent*
Key 1	*South America*	*Key 2*	*France*
Key 2	*Europe*	*Key 3*	*Canada*
Key 2	*Australia*	*Key 3*	*Greenland*
Key 3	*North America*	*Key 4*	*India*

And the same query gives different results when the table positions are swapped.

```
Right_Data_Table
| join kind=innerunique Left_Data_Table
  on $left.RightKey == $right.LeftKey
```

Left_Data_Table		***Right_Data_Table***	
LeftKey	*Continent*	*RightKey*	*Continent*
Key 1	*South America*	*Key 2*	*France*
Key 2	*Europe*	*Key 3*	*Canada*
Key 2	*Australia*	*Key 3*	*Greenland*
Key 3	*North America*	*Key 4*	*India*

So, the bottom line is the table or dataset mentioned in the left hand side is compare to unique values.

- The next type is inner join. Here is the query for the above-mentioned data tables.

```
Left_Data_Table
| join kind=inner Right_Data_Table
  on $left.LeftKey == $right.RightKey
```

As a result,

Left_Data_Table		***Right_Data_Table***	
LeftKey	*Continent*	*RightKey*	*Continent*
Key 1	*South America*	*Key 2*	*France*
Key 2	*Europe*	*Key 3*	*Canada*
Key 2	*Australia*	*Key 3*	*Greenland*
Key 3	*North America*	*Key 4*	*India*

- The next type of join is leftouter. Here is the query for the above-mentioned data tables.

Left_Data_Table | join kind= leftouter

Right_Data_Table on $left.LeftKey == $right.RightKey

As a result,

Left_Data_Table		***Right_Data_Table***	
LeftKey	*Continent*	*RightKey*	*Continent*
Key 1	*South America*	*Key 2*	*France*
Key 2	*Europe*	*Key 3*	*Canada*
Key 2	*Australia*	*Key 3*	*Greenland*
Key 3	*North America*	*Key 4*	*India*

- The next type of join is **rightouter**,
  Here is the query for the above mentioned data tables.

Left_Data_Table | join kind= rightouter

Right_Data_Table on $left.LeftKey == $right.RightKey

As a result,

Left_Data_Table		***Right_Data_Table***	
LeftKey	*Continent*	*RightKey*	*Continent*
Key 1	*South America*	*Key 2*	*France*
Key 2	*Europe*	*Key 3*	*Canada*
Key 2	*Australia*	*Key 3*	*Greenland*

Key 3	*North America*	*Key 4*	*India*

➢ The next type of join is **fullouter**,
Here is the query for the above-mentioned data tables.

Left_Data_Table | join kind=fullouter

Right_Data_Table on $left.LeftKey == $right.RightKey

As a result,

Left_Data_Table		***Right_Data_Table***	
LeftKey	*Continent*	*RightKey*	*Continent*
Key 1	*South America*	*Key 2*	*France*
Key 2	*Europe*	*Key 3*	*Canada*
Key 2	*Australia*	*Key 3*	*Greenland*
Key 3	*North America*	*Key 4*	*India*

➢ The next type of join is **leftanti**,
Here is the query for the above-mentioned data tables.

Left_Data_Table | join kind= leftanti

Right_Data_Table on $left.LeftKey == $right.RightKey

As a result,

Left_Data_Table		***Right_Data_Table***	
LeftKey	*Continent*	*RightKey*	*Continent*
Key 1	*South America*	*Key 2*	*France*
Key 2	*Europe*	*Key 3*	*Canada*
Key 2	*Australia*	*Key 3*	*Greenland*
Key 3	*North America*	*Key 4*	*India*

➢ The next type of join is **rightanti**,
Here is the query for the above-mentioned data tables.

Left_Data_Table | join kind= rightanti

Right_Data_Table on $left.LeftKey == $right.RightKey

As a result,

Left_Data_Table		***Right_Data_Table***	
LeftKey	*Continent*	*RightKey*	*Continent*
Key 1	*South America*	*Key 2*	*France*
Key 2	*Europe*	*Key 3*	*Canada*
Key 2	*Australia*	*Key 3*	*Greenland*
Key 3	*North America*	*Key 4*	*India*

➢ The next type of join is **leftsemi**,

Here is the query for the above-mentioned data tables.

Left_Data_Table | join kind= leftsemi

Right_Data_Table on $left.LeftKey == $right.RightKey

As a result,

Left_Data_Table		***Right_Data_Table***	
LeftKey	*Continent*	*RightKey*	*Continent*
Key 1	*South America*	*Key 2*	*France*
Key 2	*Europe*	*Key 3*	*Canada*
Key 2	*Australia*	*Key 3*	*Greenland*
Key 3	*North America*	*Key 4*	*India*

➢ The next type of join is **rightsemi**,

Here is the query for the above-mentioned data tables.

Left_Data_Table | join kind= rightsemi

Right_Data_Table on $left.LeftKey == $right.RightKey

As a result,

Left_Data_Table		***Right_Data_Table***	
LeftKey	*Continent*	*RightKey*	*Continent*
Key 1	*South America*	*Key 2*	*France*
Key 2	*Europe*	*Key 3*	*Canada*
Key 2	*Australia*	*Key 3*	*Greenland*

Key 3	*North America*	*Key 4*	*India*

- Now, let's look at the other possibilities of using a joins, we can apply where conditions in with joins

```
Left_Data_Table | where Continent contains "Europe"
| join kind= inner Right_Data_Table
  on $left.LeftKey == $right.RightKey
```

As a result

Left_Data_Table		***Right_Data_Table***	
LeftKey	*Continent*	*RightKey*	*Continent*
Key 1	*South America*	*Key 2*	*France*
Key 2	*Europe*	*Key 3*	*Canada*
Key 2	*Australia*	*Key 3*	*Greenland*
Key 3	*North America*	*Key 4*	*India*

- We can also use sub queries in joins

```
Left_Data_Table | where Continent in
(toscalar(Left_Data_Table | where Continent contains "Europe" | distinct Continent))
| join kind= inner
Right_Data_Table
  on $left.LeftKey == $right.RightKey
```

As a result

Left_Data_Table		***Right_Data_Table***	
LeftKey	*Continent*	*RightKey*	*Continent*
Key 1	*South America*	*Key 2*	*France*
Key 2	*Europe*	*Key 3*	*Canada*
Key 2	*Australia*	*Key 3*	*Greenland*
Key 3	*North America*	*Key 4*	*India*

Please scan the qr below for a demo

*In Summary, **join** is key word with a huge variety of option and with practice we learn the better use of them.*

SUMMARIZE FOR PERSPECTIVE

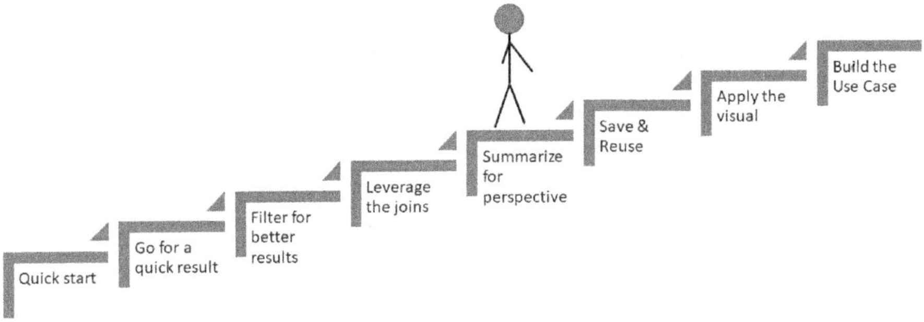

◆ ◆ ◆

Till now, we can get the dataset and join multiple tables to arrive at a result for a particular query. Next chapter "Summarize for perspective" is about getting a perspective, a perspective helps to look at our results set for different possibilities. For example, we have a query written to get all the logs for a user across SigninLogs & NonInteractive SigInlogs.

The objective of this chapter to provide us a different perspective.

After that, if we investigate a various set of data like count failed login for that user, count of successful login for that user. Furthermore, the applications user is using the most. Those kinds of results will give us a different perspective to look at and also gain an extended knowledge about our results.

As we continue our journey through advanced data analysis in KQL, building upon the techniques explored in previous chapters, we now shift our focus to the relevance of summarization. By concentrating large volumes of data into meaningful summaries, we can gain valuable insights and a broader perspective on our security landscape.

In the realm of cybersecurity, the ability to summarize and aggregate data is invaluable. Summarization allows us to uncover trends, patterns and statistical information that may not be apparent in individual records. In this chapter, we explore the art of summarizing data using KQL within Microsoft Sentinel. By employing techniques such as aggregation functions and transforming data into meaningful representations, we can derive valuable perspectives that inform decision-making and drive effective security strategies.

The objective of this chapter is to help us to understand on how to leverage the summarization in KQL. We will delve into various techniques to summarize datasets, including the use of aggregation functions, make_list and make_set.

By the end of this chapter, we will have a comprehensive understanding of how to extract valuable insights from our data by condensing it into meaningful summaries. So, let's get started with this chapter and know more about the possibility of a building perspectives.

◆ ◆ ◆

Summarize our dataset to get an overview

Once we have the basic query steps mentioned in the previous chapters

➢ At the very first, we want to summarize based on some specific columns.
For example, we want to summarize on UserPrinciapalName, AppDisplayName wit the below query

SigninLogs | summarize by UserPrincipalName, AppDisplayName

As a result, we will be able to see a unique combination of UserPrinciapalName, AppDisplayName.
Now, this can also be achieved using distinct. But, to apply a real summary with a count added to each by using the below query.

SigninLogs | summarize count() by UserPrincipalName, AppDisplayName

And the result will display the same.

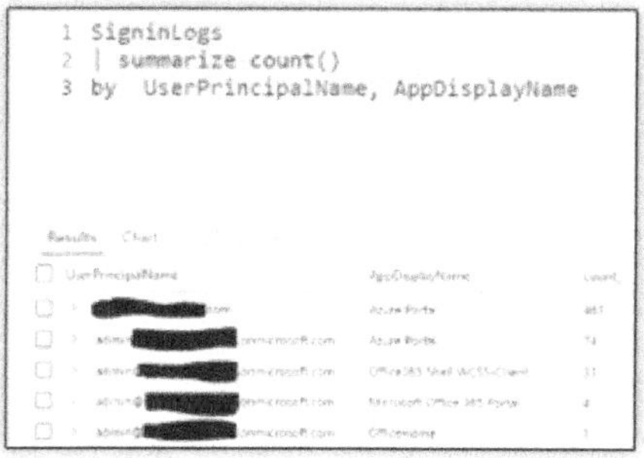

➢ Next, we can find out more than one aggregation using summarize.
For example, if we want to get the minimum and maximum time from SigninLogs we can use the below query.

SigninLogs | summarize min(TimeGenerated), max(TimeGenerated)

As a result, we will be able to see the maximum and minimum timeframe.

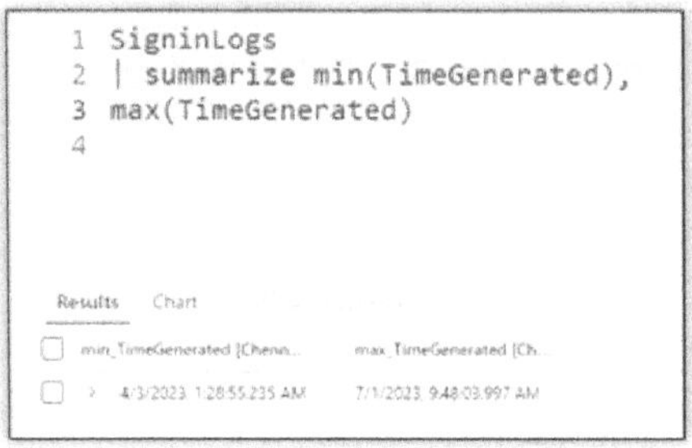

➢ Next, we can add up both concepts.
For example, we want to find the minimum and maximum Time a user has signed in we can use the below query:

SigninLogs | summarize min(TimeGenerated),max(TimeGenerated) by UserPrincipalName

And as a result, the query displays the min and max TimeGenerated for each user.

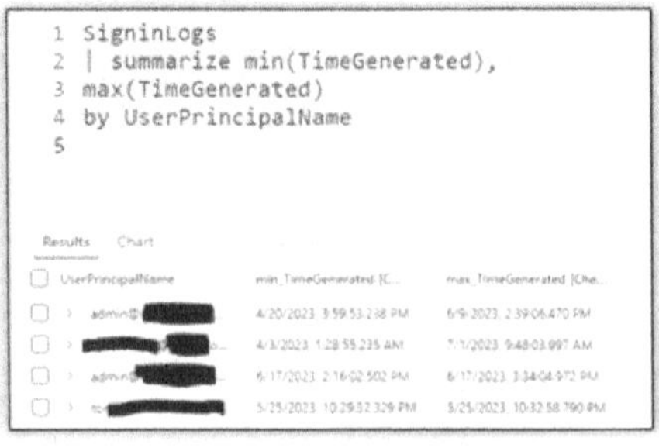

Please scan the qr below for a demo

So, summarize can be used for different to get different perspective from the dataset.

Apply make_list to summarize all values

Make_list is used in conjunction with summarize operator. This can be used for one or more than one column. This can also be combined with a multiple other functions like bin.

➢ We can use this with only one expression

For example, we want to make a list of the users from SigninLogs, we can use the below query

SigninLogs | summarize make_list(UserPrincipalName)

And the result is

➢ We might think this list is huge, then we can define the number of results.

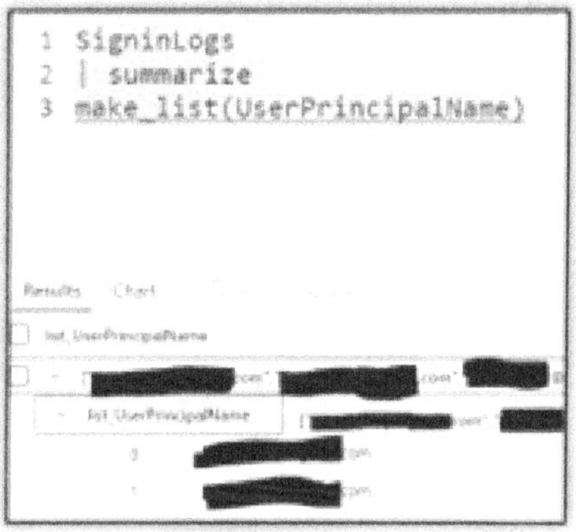

For example, we can use the below query, the maximum number which is default as well is 1048576

SigninLogs | summarize make_list(UserPrincipalName,3)

And the result is

➢ Next, adding more to the query

SigninLogs | summarize make_list(UserPrincipalName) by ResultType

And the result is

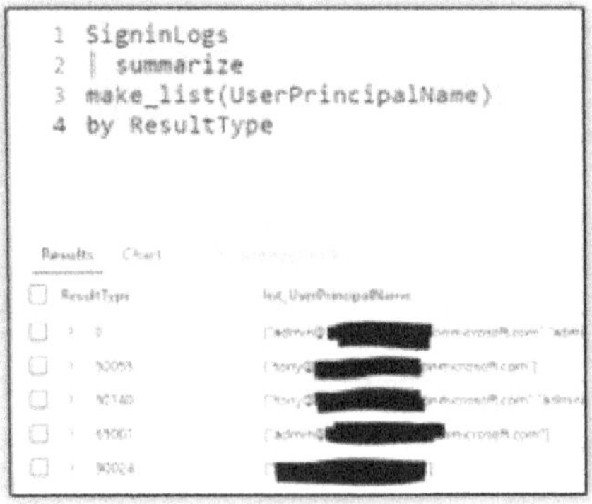

➢ Next, keep adding more columns to the query.

For example, if we want to add AppDisplayName, we can use the below query

SigninLogs | summarize make_list(UserPrincipalName)

by ResultType, AppDisplayName

And the result is

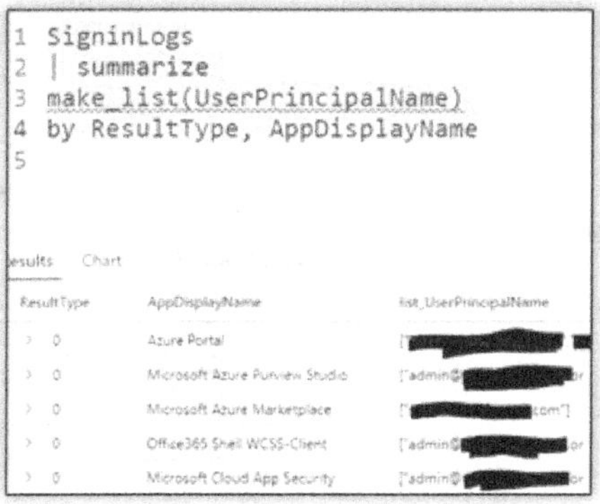

➢ Next, we can segment the results by bin as well.
For example, if we want to list the list user for every 24 hours us can use the below query

SigninLogs | summarize make_list(UserPrincipalName)
by ResultType, bin(TimeGenerated,24h)

And the result is

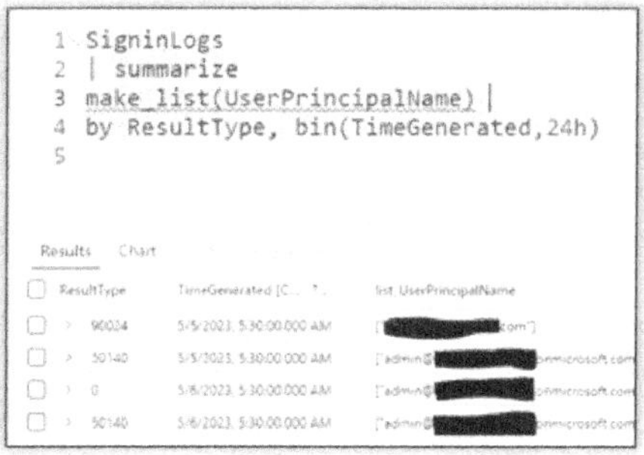

➢ Now, bring it altogether by limiting the list. We can use the below query
SigninLogs | summarize make_list(UserPrincipalName,1)
by ResultType, bin(TimeGenerated,24h)

And the result is

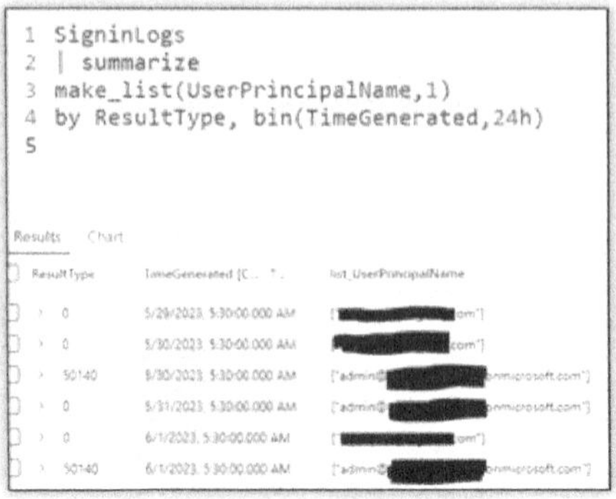

Please scan the qr below for a demo

In summary, using make_list we can do the folllwing

- ✓ *Find out the list of results.*
- ✓ *Use the list with other operators like count*
- ✓ *Get a list of the dataset, if the right combination is used.*

◆ ◆ ◆

Apply make_set to summarize unique values

◆ ◆ ◆

Make_set is used in conjunction with summarize operator. This can be used for one or more than one column. This can also be combined with a multiple other functions like bin.

➢ Similar to make_list, make_set can be used for a single

For example, we want to make a list of the users from SigninLogs, we can use the below query

SigninLogs | summarize make_set(UserPrincipalName)

And the result is

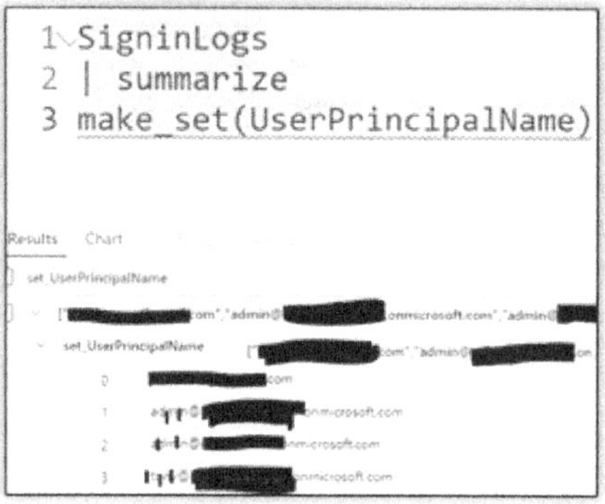

➢ We might think this list is huge, then we can define the number of results.

For example, we can use the below query, the maximum number which is default as well is 1048576

SigninLogs | summarize make_set(UserPrincipalName,3)

And the result is

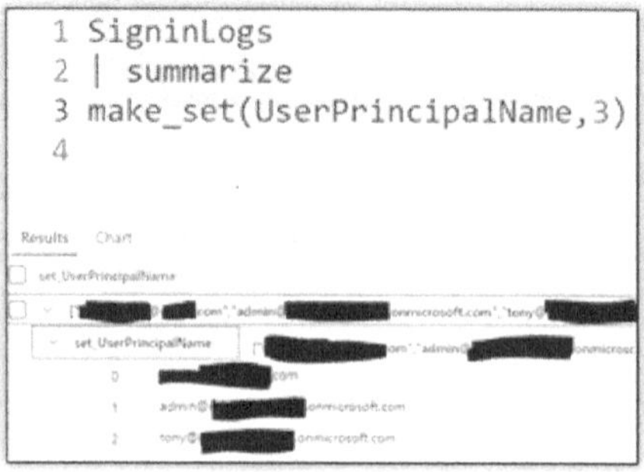

➢ Next, adding more to the query

SigninLogs | summarize make_set(UserPrincipalName) by ResultType

And the result is

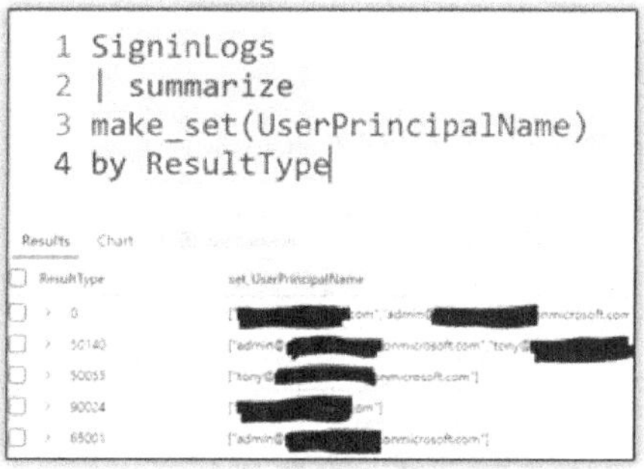

➢ Next, keep adding more columns to the query.

For example, if we want to add app display name we can use the below query

SigninLogs | summarize make_set(UserPrincipalName) by ResultType, AppDisplayName

And the result is

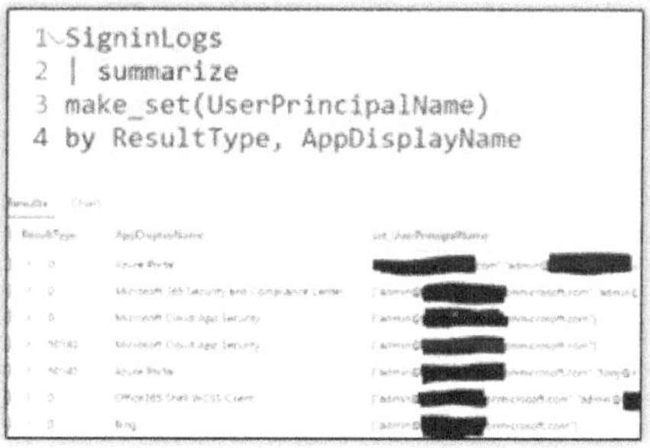

➢ Next, we can segment the results by bin as well.

For example, we want to list the list user for every 24 hours then we can use the below query

SigninLogs | summarize make_set(UserPrincipalName)

by ResultType, bin(TimeGenerated,24h)

And the result is

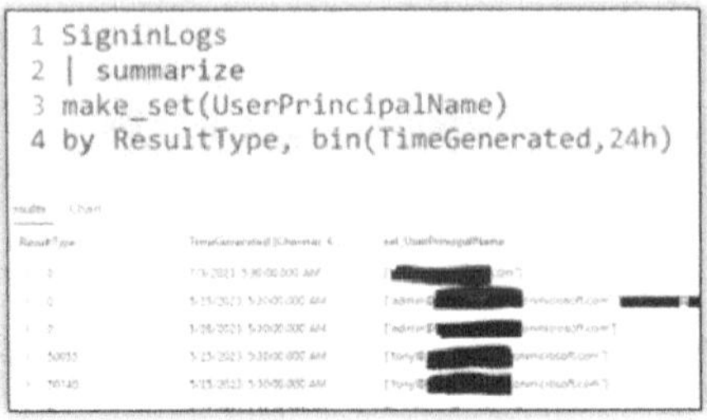

Please scan the qr below for a demo

In summary, using make_set we can do the folllwing:

✓ *Find out the unique results.*

✓ *Use the uniqueness with other operators like count*

✓ *Get a summary of the dataset, if the right combination is used.*

◆ ◆ ◆

SAVE & REUSE

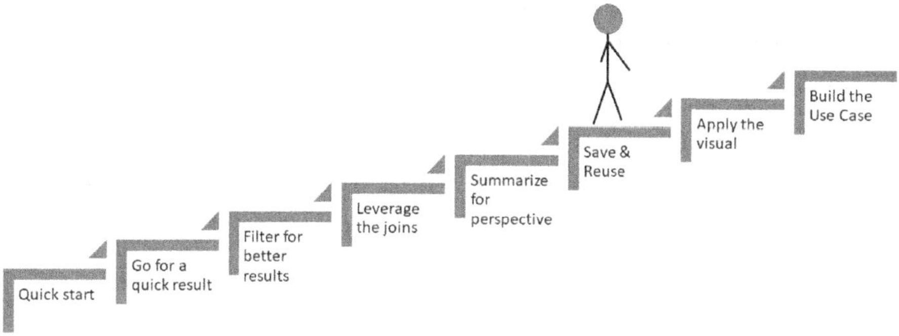
Quick start
Go for a quick result
Filter for better results
Leverage the joins
Summarize for perspective
Save & Reuse
Apply the visual
Build the Use Case

◆ ◆ ◆

Building upon the knowledge gained in the previous chapters, where we explored advanced techniques for data analysis and summarization using KQL, we now turn our attention to the importance of saving and reusing queries. By effectively managing and organizing our queries, we can enhance productivity, promote collaboration and streamline data analysis workflows.

A function can be saved with some input parameters too where it acts as dynamic query and displays results based on query parameter provided.

As a security analyst or administrator, we often come across recurring scenarios where we need to perform similar queries or execute complex functions repeatedly. The ability to save and reuse our queries not only saves time and effort but also ensures consistency and accuracy in our analysis. So, we will learn about the methods of saving queries and functions in Microsoft Sentinel for increased productivity and efficiency.

The objective of this chapter is to provide the knowledge and steps required to save and reuse our queries effectively in Microsoft Sentinel. We will navigate through the process of saving our queries, organizing them for easy access and retrieving and executing them when needed.

Throughout this chapter, we will cover the following sub-topics:

Saving and organizing our queries for efficient access and reuse
Executing saved queries and leveraging query history for quick retrieval
Creating and utilizing functions to encapsulate reusable blocks of code.
Sharing and collaborating with others by exporting and importing queries and functions.
Best practices and tips for effective query and function management in Microsoft Sentinel.

The ability to save and reuse our queries and functions in Microsoft Sentinel offers significant benefits to our security operations. By eliminating the need to recreate complex queries from scratch, we can save time, ensure consistency in our analysis and focus on generating actionable insights. Also, sharing queries and functions facilitates collaboration among team members, promoting knowledge sharing and enabling efficient teamwork.

So, let's get started with this chapter and know more about the possibility of a saving & reusing.

◆ ◆ ◆

Save our query

◆ ◆ ◆

Once the query is complete, we can save that in the context of a log analytics workspace or in any other query packs. And here are the steps to do this:

➢ Start writing our query and run them to verify the results are as expected and optimized.

For example, we try to write a query to understand the percentage of Signins and it might look like this

```
SigninLogs
| summarize Total = count(),
FailedSignIns = countif(ResultType !=0),
SuccessfulSignIns = countif(ResultType ==0)
by UserPrincipalName
| extend ["Failed %"] = (FailedSignIns * 1.00/Total) * 100
| extend ["Success %"] = (FailedSignIns * 1.00/Total) * 100
```

And this gives us the desired the result.

➢ As a next step, we need to save the query using Save as query option.

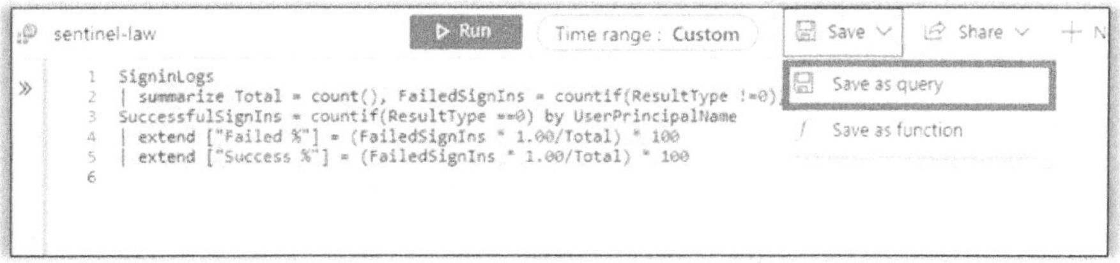

➢ Further, it will open a new slider in the right side for us to fill in the details

And once we fill in the

Query Name

Description

Save as a legacy query Path-> Save to default query pack. Tags

Resource Type ->

Category ->

Label ->

Hit the save button and wait the conformation to ensure the query is saved successfully.

The Notification

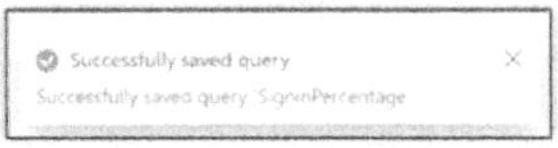

Change the query tab

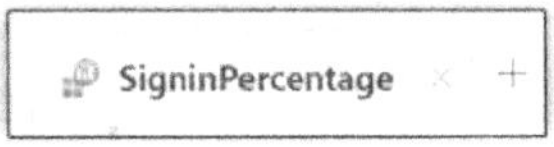

These 2 indicate that our query is saved.

➢ As a continuation, we need to test the saved query too.
Now, use the left navigation to fins the saved query.
Once found, click on a to see the query in action and it should give us the results.

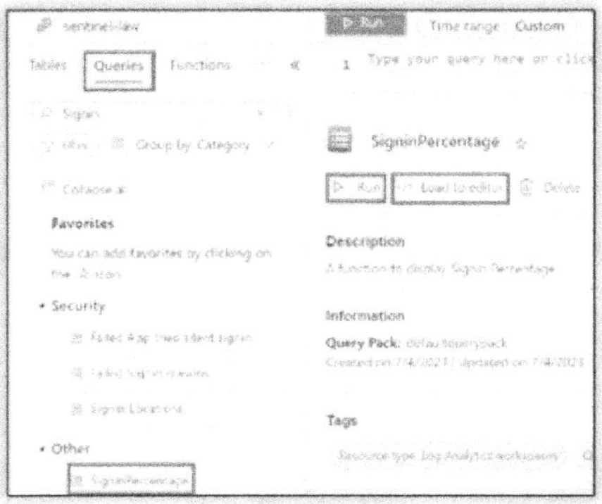

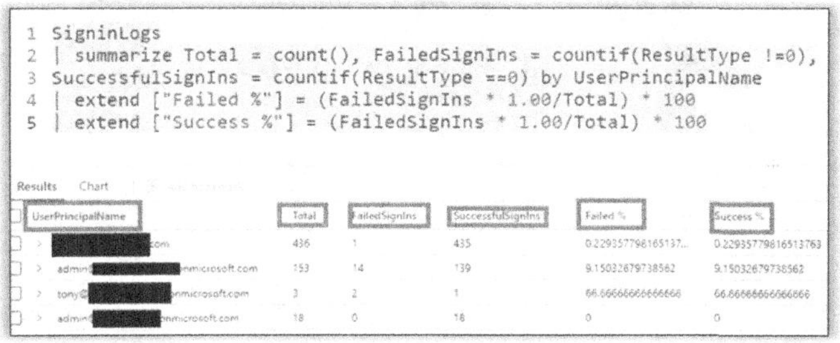

Once a query is saved it will be accessible by everyone who has read access to the workspace at the minimum.

This feature will be very helpful when we have a complex query which is needed to use either daily or every now & then, like Signin Percentage, List of Machines not checked-in for last 24 hours etc.

Please scan the qr below for a demo

Save as a function

Saving a query as a function is a step ahead than saving as query. The best time to save a query as a function is when we are not worried about the logic underlying or maybe we need to have a parser created where we would like to keep the logic abstracted. Or cases, where we want to call a complex query with a simplified and easy to understand alias.

Here are the steps to achieve this:

➢ As a first step, write the query in an efficient & optimized way ensure the fastest results.

➢ Once the query is tested and ready to be saved, the query need to be saved as a function an at the same time the query needs to be parametrized if any parameter are used

For example:

SigninLogs | where UserPrincipalName contains GivenName

| summarize Total = count(),FailedSignIns = countif(ResultType !=0),

SuccessfulSignIns = countif(ResultType ==0)

by UserPrincipalName

| extend ["Failed %"] = (FailedSignIns * 1.00/Total) * 100

| extend ["Success %"] = (FailedSignIns * 1.00/Total) * 100

| render timechart

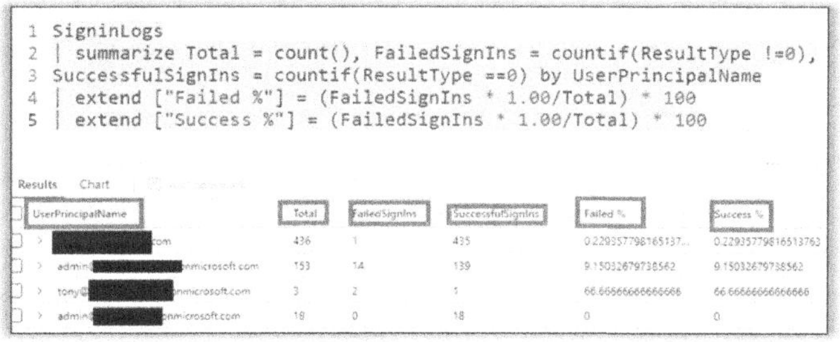

➢ Further, it will open a new slider in the right side for us to fill in the details

Function Name -> will be the function alias.

Legacy Category -> Provide a category name

Parameters -> This is a unique feature where we can pass some parameters to have the query dynamic.

e.g. - GivenName is defined as string parameter to use the function with some a parameter.

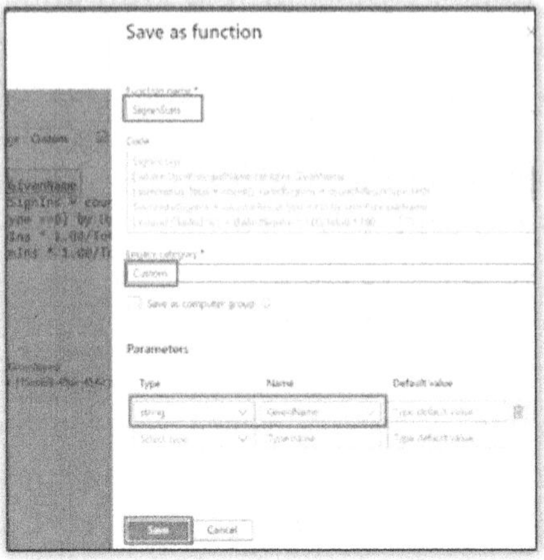

Hit the save button and wait the conformation to ensure the query is saved successfully.
The notification

and the change in query tab name.

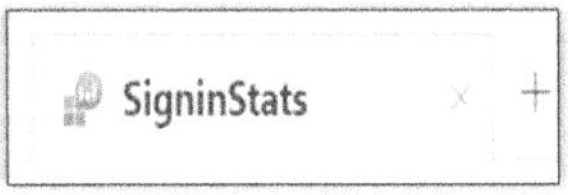

These 2 indicates that our query is saved.
As a continuation, we need to test the saved function too. Now, use the left navigation to find the saved function.

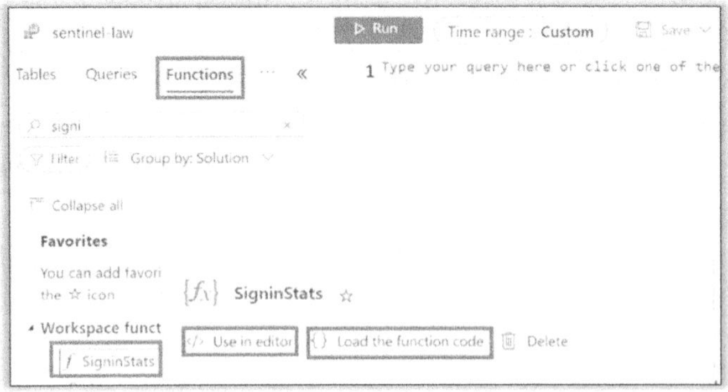

➢ Once found, click on Use in Editor see the function query in action and it should give us the results

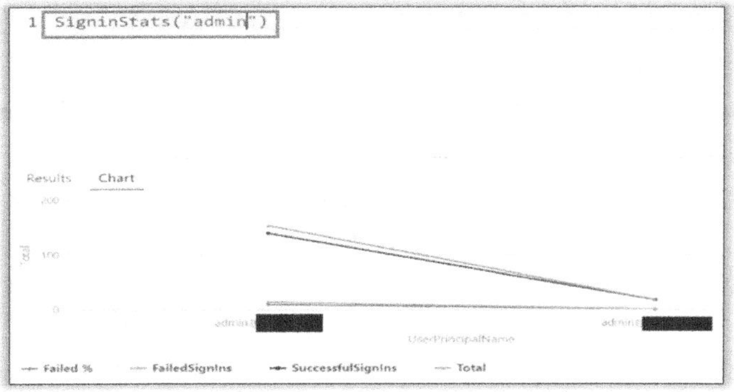

Once a query is saved it will be accessible by everyone who has read access to the workspace at the minimum.

This feature will be very helpful when we have a complex data set ingested and we need to write parser or we need a particular statistics with some parameters.

Now, it is also important to know to use what.

Please scan the qr below for a demo

When to save a function

Reusability: When we save a query as a function in KQL, we can reuse it across different queries or workspaces. Functions encapsulate a specific logic or operation, allowing us to modularize our code and promote code reusability.

Parameterization: Functions in KQL can accept parameters, which allows for flexibility and customization. By passing different values to the parameters, we can reuse the same function with varying inputs, making our code more versatile.

Code organization: Saving queries as functions helps maintain a clean and organized codebase. Functions can be stored in a separate module or file, making it easier to manage and locate specific pieces of code. This promotes code readability and maintainability.

Encapsulation: Functions enable encapsulation of complex operations or calculations. By creating a function, we can abstract away the implementation details and focus on the higher-level logic. This promotes code abstraction and makes the queries more concise and readable.

Code sharing: Functions can be shared with other team members or the wider community. We can create a library of functions that address common use cases or solve specific problems, promoting collaboration and knowledge sharing.

When to save as a query

Simplicity: Saving a query as is without converting it into a function offers simplicity and quick execution. It is useful for ad-hoc or one-time queries that do not require reusability or parameterization.

Immediate execution: Saving a query directly allows us to execute it immediately without the need to call a function. This can be convenient for quick data exploration or troubleshooting scenarios.

Query-specific logic: When we save a query as is, we can include specific logic or calculations within the query itself. This approach is suitable when the logic is tied directly to the query and does not need to be reused across multiple queries.

Query history tracking: By saving queries individually, we can keep track of the execution history and easily refer to previous queries. This can be helpful for auditing purposes or revisiting past analyses.

Learning and experimentation: Saving queries individually allows for experimentation and learning. As we explore different query structures and techniques, saving them as separate queries helps us to track and compare the results.

APPLY THE VISUAL

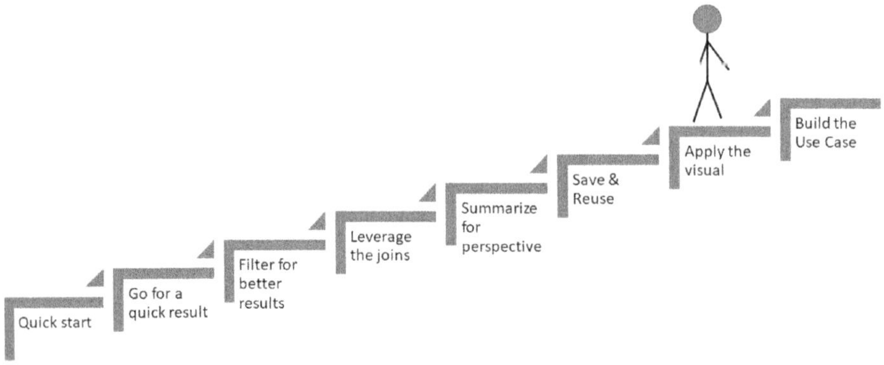

On top of the learning from the previous chapters, we will learn about visualization of data using KQL queries and explore various techniques to present our data in visually engaging formats. Whether it's line charts, bar charts or pie charts, we will learn how to create dynamic visualizations that highlight critical information and help us make informed decisions.

The objective of this chapter is to understand how to effectively visualize data not only enhances the presentation of our findings but also enables us to communicate complex security-related information to stakeholders and decision-makers in a concise and impactful manner. By utilizing the visualization capabilities of KQL, we can transform the data into visual narratives that tell compelling stories and drive actionable insights.

Throughout this chapter, we will cover the fundamentals of data visualization, including selecting the appropriate chart types, customizing visual elements and applying filters to focus on specific data subsets. We will explore practical examples and demonstrate how to leverage KQL queries to generate visualizations that provide meaningful insights into our security data.

By the end of this chapter, we will have a solid understanding of how to apply visualization techniques using KQL in Microsoft Sentinel. We will be equipped with the knowledge and skills to transform raw security data into visually compelling representations and empower to effectively analyze and communicate security insights. So, let's learn the application of visuals with KQL in Microsoft Sentinel.

Apply visual on the dataset

◆ ◆ ◆

A visual is a thousand times better than a query returning results in a tabular structure. A visual give of an edge over our results. And in this chapter, we will learn how to convert a query to visual result.

Now, to apply visual to a query first we need to have a query which is

Written for a purpose.
Provides the desired results.
Applied to a particular time frame.
Gives a perspective about the data.

And as the visuals are 2 dimensional, we need to identify the columns (one or more at times) to be placed in X-axis & Y-Axis respectively.

Here are available visuals:

- ➢ Pie chart
- ➢ Bar chat
- ➢ Column Chart
- ➢ Scatter Chart
- ➢ Time chart

Every chat has its own purpose and should be used within that scope.

Pie Chart: A pie chart typically represents numbers in percentages, used to visualize a part to whole relationship or a composition. Pie charts are not meant to compare individual sections to each other or to represent exact values.

For example, we can get the PIE chart out of CrossTenantAccessType from SigninLogs using the below query:

SigninLogs | summarize count() by CrossTenantAccessType | render piechart

To be used best for

➢ The total sum of all segments equals 100 percent. ➢ If we do not have more than 4 or 5 categories, it is even better to have only 2 categories.

➢ There is a clear category us want to focus on. Not to be used in case we have 2 or more categories as same.

And the result will look like

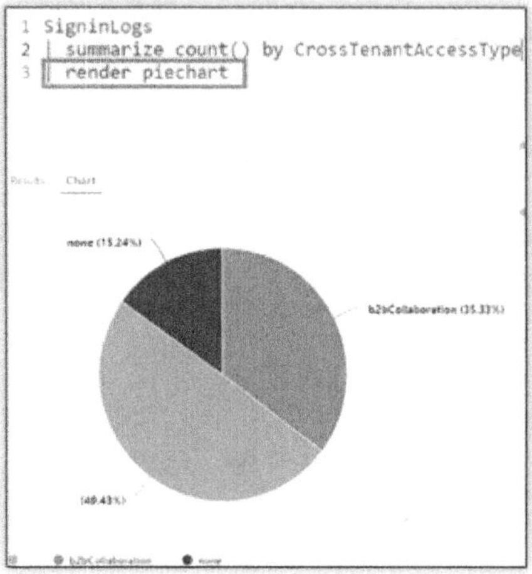

Bar Chart and Column Charts : Column and bar charts are used to compare different items or show a comparison of items over time. Bars on a column chart are vertical, while bars on a bar chart are horizontal. Bar charts are generally used to help avoid clutter when one data label is long or if we have more than 10 items to compare. Bar charts can also display negative numbers. For example, we can draw a bar or column chart with ResultType from SigninLogs

SigninLogs | summarize count() by ResultType | render barchart

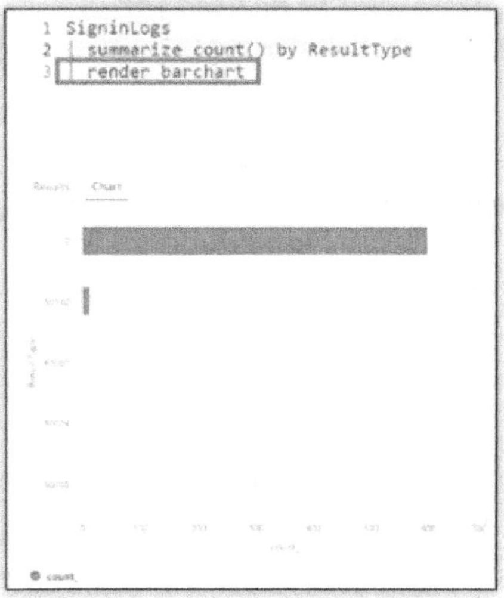

SigninLogs | summarize count() by ResultType | render columnchart

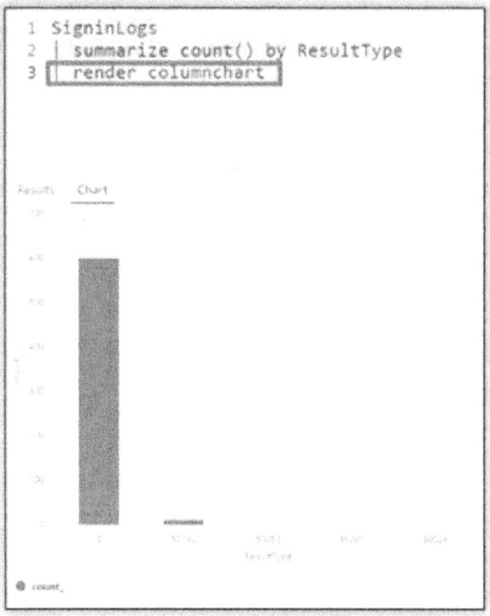

<u>To be used best for</u>

Start the y-axis at zero. Our eyes are sensitive to the area of bars on a chart. If those bars are truncated, the viewer might draw the wrong conclusions.

Label the axes. Labeling the axes gives our viewer context.

Put value labels on bars. This helps to preserve the clean lines of the bar lengths.

Not to be used for

Use too many colors. Avoid the 'rainbow effect.' Using a single color, or varying shades of the same color is a much better practice.

We can highlight one bar in particular if that is serve the clean lines of the bar lengths. Not to be used for Use too many colors. Avoid the 'rainbow effect.' Using a single color, or varying shades of the same color is a much better practice. We can highlight one bar in particular if that is the message we want to get across.

Scatter Chart: Scatter plots, a lot like line graphs, use horizontal and vertical axes to plot data points. But scatter plots have a unique purpose – they show how one variable affects another, meaning we can visualize distribution, relationships and trends in our data.

For example, we can draw a scatter chart for the count of AppDisplayName in SigninLogs

SigninLogs | summarize count() by AppDisplayName | render scatterchart

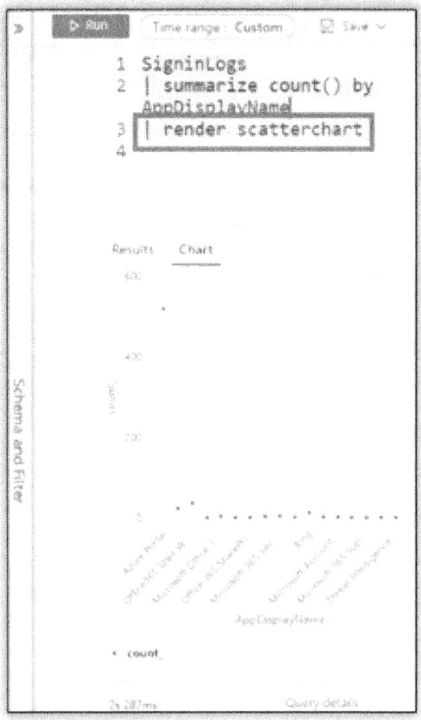

To be used best for

Use scatter plots when we have a lot of data. Scatter plots lend themselves to large data sets.

Use regression lines to guess Y if we have X. Helpful when estimating certain unknown data points.

Start the Y-axis at 0. If we set the Y-axis above 0 it skews the way our graph looks and our data won't be presented accurately.

Not to be used best for

Use scatter plots when we have a lot of data. Scatter plots lend themselves to large data sets.

Use regression lines to guess Y if we have X. Helpful when estimating certain unknown data points.

Start the Y-axis at 0. If we set the Y-axis above 0 it skews the way our graph looks and our data won't be presented accurately.

Time Chart: The timeline chart is a variation of line charts.

Obviously, any line chart that shows values over a period is a timeline chart. The only difference is in functionality, it will let us see the time axis to see more details or overall trends.
For example , getting the user signin count for each day.

SigninLogs

| summarize count() by UserPrincipalName,bin(TimeGenerated,24h)

| render timechart

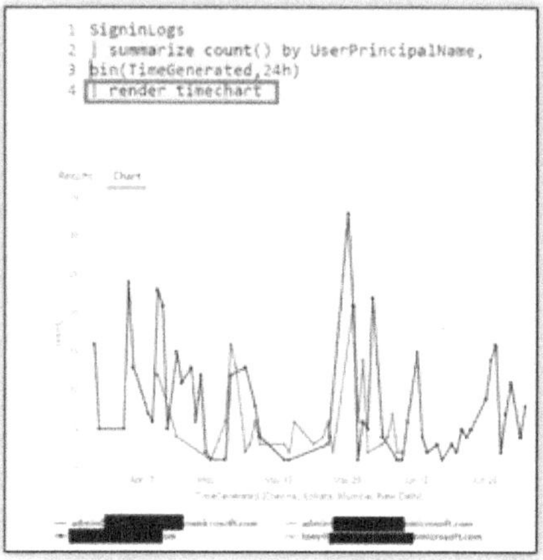

<u>To be used best for</u>

Use lines to represent continuous data with an equal interval.
Time should always be plotted from left to right.
The axis might start from a non-zero segment if the intended message of the chart is the rate of change or overall trend, not exact values, or comparison. There is a clear category us want to focus on.

<u>Not to be used</u>

when multiple intervals are used.

Please scan the qr below for a demo

In summary, each visual has solves a particular purpose and we choose the visual carefully to convey the data.

◆ ◆ ◆

BUILD THE USE CASE

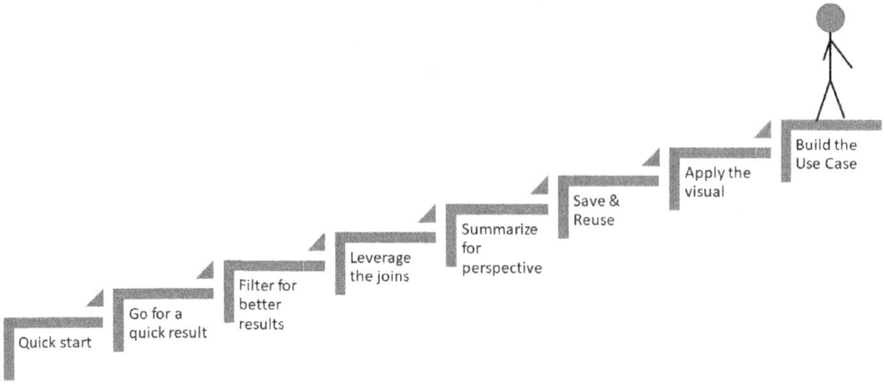

◆ ◆ ◆

After we have gone through the workflow of building a query, as the ultimate scope we will be building the Use case where we perform an exercise to embark on an exciting journey of building impactful use cases using the power of KQL and visualizations in Microsoft Sentinel.

The objective of this chapter is to equip us with the skills and knowledge necessary to build a comprehensive use case using KQL and visualizations. By following the step-by-step process and leveraging the various techniques discussed, we will be able to extract valuable insights from the data and drive actionable outcomes.

Building a use case is not just about extracting data; it is about transforming information into actionable intelligence. By following the process outlined in this chapter, we will have the method to address specific security challenges, detect anomalies, investigate incidents and make data-driven decisions that enhance our organization's overall security posture.

In this chapter, we will explore the systematic approach to transform raw data into actionable insights by formulating hypotheses, writing queries, refining results, summarizing data, applying joins if necessary and ultimately constructing a final query that uncovers valuable information to address our specific use case.

Formulating hypotheses by defining the investigative goals and objectives to guide our analysis.

Writing queries to construct KQL queries to retrieve specific data points aligned with our use case.

Refining results by applying filters, aggregations and advanced functions to enhance the accuracy and relevance of our query output.

Summarizing data to gain high-level overviews and identify patterns within our dataset.

Applying joins if necessary to Correlate data from multiple datasets using common fields to uncover valuable relationships and insights.

Visualizing our findings through dynamic visualizations, charts and dashboards to effectively communicate our analysis results.

Get ready to embark on a journey of building impactful use cases using KQL and visualizations. By the end of this chapter,

A use case is basically a set of one or more than one KQL query to establish a particular hypothesis or a business case.

We will elaborate about 3 more use cases though out the chapter.

- ➢ *Brute force in SigninLogs*
- ➢ *Analyze the noise in non-interactive SigninLogs*
- ➢ *Deviation of Security Events across windows devices.*

By the end of this chapter, we will possess the knowledge and expertise to extract valuable insights from our data, construct comprehensive queries and present our findings in visually engaging ways, taking our security analysis and decision-making capabilities to new heights with through the defined model of use case building. So, let's get started with this chapter and by building some use cases.

◆ ◆ ◆

Brute force in Signin logs

The Hypotheses

A simple brute force attack occurs when a hacker attempts to guess a user's login credentials manually without using any software. This is typically through standard password combinations or personal identification number (PIN) codes.

The Dataset

As we are trying the find a credential compromise, we the first data set should be the SigninLogs.

The Workflow

We begin with a search

```
SigninLogs | search ResultType != 0
```

⬇

Project the necessary columns

```
SigninLogs
| search ResultType != 0
| project UserPrincipalName, ResultType, TimeGenerated, Location, IPAddress
```

Extend for more details

⬇

```
SigninLogs
| search ResultType != 0
| project UserPrincipalName, ResultType, TimeGenerated, Location, IPAddress
| extend latitude_ = tostring(parse_json(tostring(LocationDetails.geoCoordinates)).latitude)
| extend longitude_ = tostring(parse_json(tostring(LocationDetails.geoCoordinates)).longitude)
```

⬇

See the count

```
SigninLogs
| search ResultType != 0
| project UserPrincipalName, ResultType, TimeGenerated, Location, IPAddress
| extend latitude_ = tostring(parse_json(tostring(LocationDetails.geoCoordinates)).latitude)
| extend longitude_ = tostring(parse_json(tostring(LocationDetails.geoCoordinates)).longitude)|
| count
```

⬇

Find unique values

```
SigninLogs
| search ResultType != 0
| project UserPrincipalName, ResultType, TimeGenerated, Location, IPAddress
```

```
| extend latitude_ = tostring(parse_json(tostring(LocationDetails.geoCoordinates)).latitude)
| extend longitude_ = tostring(parse_json(tostring(LocationDetails.geoCoordinates)).longitude)
| distinct UserPrincipalName, longitude_, latitude_, IPAddress
```

The Final Query

```
SigninLogs
| summarize arg_max(TimeGenerated, ResultType), FailedLogin = countif(ResultType != 0) by UserPrincipalName, bin(TimeGenerated,1h)
```

Please scan the qr below for a demo

Analyze the Noise in non-interactive Signin logs

signins
failed
noninteractive

The Hypotheses:

This use case purely based on some which do not see with open eyes.

It is about understanding the dataset for all the non-interactive signins into Azure AD.

The Dataset

The table name will be AADNonInteractiveUserSignInLogs

The Workflow

We begin with a search

```
AADNonInteractiveUserSignInLogs | search ResultType != 0
```

⬇

Project the necessary columns

```
AADNonInteractiveUserSignInLogs
| search ResultType != 0
| project UserPrincipalName, ResultType, TimeGenerated, Location, IPAddress
```

⬇

Extend for more details

```
AADNonInteractiveUserSignInLogs
| search ResultType != 0
| project UserPrincipalName, ResultType, TimeGenerated, Location, IPAddress
| extend latitude_ = tostring(parse_json(tostring(LocationDetails.geoCoordinates)).latitude) | extend
longitude_ = tostring(parse_json(tostring(LocationDetails.geoCoordinates)).longitude)
```

⬇

See the count

```
AADNonInteractiveUserSignInLogs
| search ResultType != 0
| project UserPrincipalName, ResultType, TimeGenerated, Location, IPAddress
| extend latitude_ = tostring(parse_json(tostring(LocationDetails.geoCoordinates)).latitude)
| extend longitude_ = tostring(parse_json(tostring(LocationDetails.geoCoordinates)).longitude)|
| count
```

⬇

Find unique values

```
AADNonInteractiveUserSignInLogs | search ResultType != 0
| project UserPrincipalName, ResultType, TimeGenerated, Location, IPAddress
| extend latitude_ = tostring(parse_json(tostring(LocationDetails.geoCoordinates)).latitude)
| extend longitude_ = tostring(parse_json(tostring(LocationDetails.geoCoordinates)).longitude)
| distinct UserPrincipalName, longitude_, latitude_, IPAddress
```

The Final Query

```
AADNonInteractiveUserSignInLogs
| extend ErrorCode = tostring(parse_json(Status).errorCode)
| summarize TotalLogins = count(),
SuccessfulLogins = countif(ErrorCode == 0),
FailedLogins = countif(ErrorCode != 0),
Users = make_set(UserPrincipalName)
by AppDisplayName, ClientAppUsed
| where FailedLogins > 0
| project UserCount = array_length(Users),AppDisplayName, ClientAppUsed
| take 10
| render columnchart
```

Please scan the qr below for an elaboration

The Result will look like

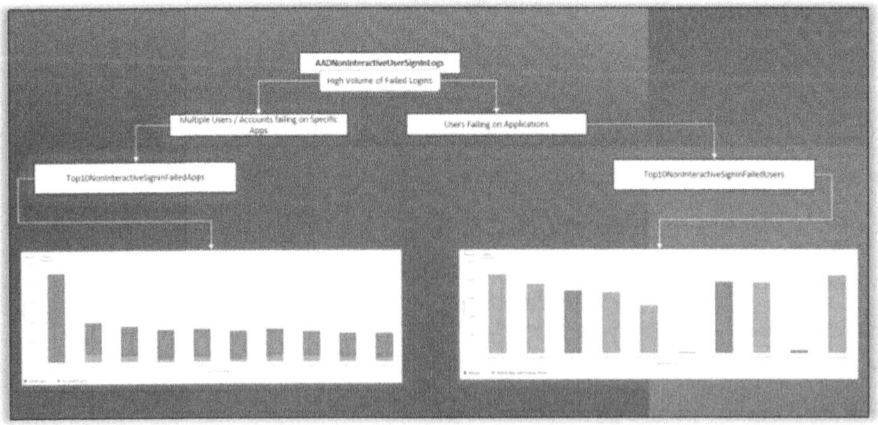

◆ ◆ ◆

Deviation in Security Events

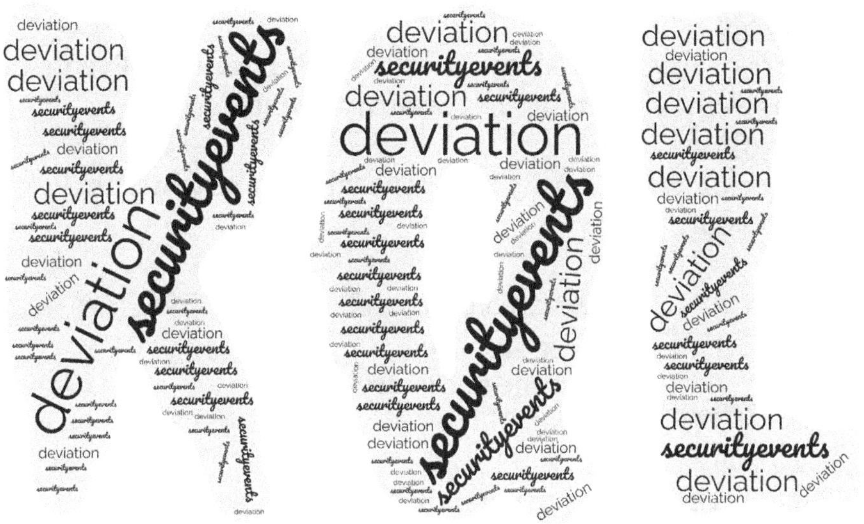

The Hypotheses

In this use case we will be discussing another interesting way. Generally, we deploy agents Microsoft Monitoring Agent & Azure Monitoring Agent to collect Security Events from the machines. Now, in this use case once all the events are collected, we will see how to identify a machine which is basically ingesting way low, or way high compared to other domain controllers.

The Dataset

As we are trying to find the details of the Security Event, the dataset is event viewer logs i.e., Security Events.

The Workflow

In this workflow we already know the table name which is Security Event.

⬇

So, the search part can be skipped.

⬇

Project the necessary columns

```
SecurityEvents | project EventID, Computer
```

⬇

Do we need to extend? does not look like?

See the count and this will also project about the detailed unique count for each computer.

```
SecurityEvents | project EventID, Computer |summarize count() by Computer
```

⬇

The Final Query

```
// Defining lookback Time.
let lookbacktime = 1h;
//Deriving the average.
let BL = toscalar(SecurityEvent | where TimeGenerated > ago(lookbacktime)
| summarize count() by Computer | summarize avg(count_));
//Fetching actual event count
SecurityEvent | where TimeGenerated > ago(lookbacktime)
| summarize count() by Computer
// Calculating the Deviation
| extend Deviation = (count_ - BL) / BL
| project-away count_
```

// rendering visual

| render columnchart

The results will look like this.

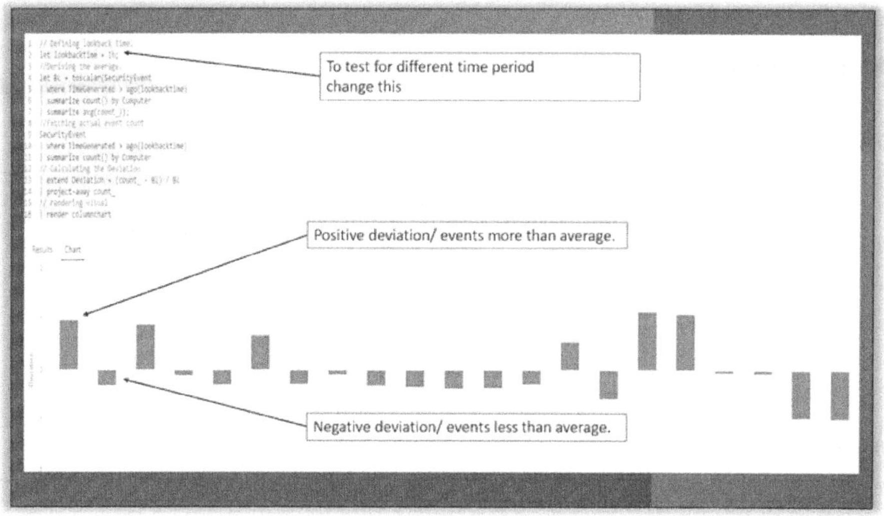

Please scan the qr below for a demo

There are some more to these use cases:

User Account Anomaly Detection:

➢ ***Hypothesis***: Identify user accounts with abnormal behavior, such as multiple failed logins attempts or unusual access patterns.

➢ ***Solution***: Write a KQL query to analyze authentication logs and detect deviations from normal user behavior. For example:

let abnormalUsers = SecurityEvent

```
| where EventID == 4625 and AccountType == "User"
| summarize FailedLoginAttempts = countif(Status == "Failure") by AccountName
| where FailedLoginAttemp
```

Data Exfiltration Monitoring:

➢ **Hypothesis**: Monitor network traffic for signs of data exfiltration or unauthorized file transfers.

➢ ***Solution***: Construct a KQL query to analyze network logs and identify suspicious outbound traffic patterns. For example:

```
let suspiciousTraffic = NetworkConnection
| where RemotePort == 443 and (RemoteIP contains "192.168.0." or RemoteIP contains "10.0.0.")
| summarize OutboundConnections = count() by Computer, RemoteIP
| where OutboundConnections > 100;
```

Malware Detection:

➢ ***Hypothesis***: Identify systems or user accounts exhibiting behaviors consistent with malware infections.

➢ ***Solution***: Write a KQL query to analyze endpoint logs and detect suspicious processes or file activities. For example:

```
let potentialMalware = SecurityEvent
| where EventID == 4688 and ProcessCommandLine has_any ("powershell.exe", "cmd.exe", "malware.exe")
| summarize Occurrences = count() by Computer, Account
| where Occurrences > 5;
```

Privilege Escalation Monitoring:

➢ ***Hypothesis***: Monitor for signs of privilege escalation attempts or suspicious elevation of user privileges.

➢ ***Solution***: Use KQL to analyze security logs and identify elevation events or suspicious privilege-related activities. For example:

```
let suspiciousElevation = SecurityEvent
| where EventID == 4672 and NewProcessName has_any ("cmd.exe", "powershell.exe")
| summarize ElevationEvents = count() by SubjectUserName
| where ElevationEvents > 5;
```

Account Enumeration Detection:

➢ ***Hypothesis***: Identify potential account enumeration attacks targeting user accounts or network services.

➢ ***Solution***: Construct a KQL query to analyze authentication logs and detect repeated failed login attempts. For example:

```
let accountEnumeration = SecurityEvent
| where EventID == 4625 and Status == "Failure" and AccountType == "User"
| summarize FailedAttempts = count() by AccountName, SourceIP
| where FailedAttempts > 10;
```

Suspicious PowerShell Command Detection:

Hypothesis: Detect suspicious or malicious PowerShell commands executed within the environment.

Solution: Write a KQL query to analyze PowerShell logs and identify potentially malicious commands. For example:

```
let suspiciousPowerShell = SecurityEvent | where EventID == 4104;
```

Please scan the qr below for a demo for some more demos:

LEARNING SUMMARY

After the completion of this book, we can build our own KQL queries.

We can understand the business case and use the framework used in this book to build the respective queries.

And once a query is being built, us can do lot more with query. We can use the queries in our detection, we can use the query for hunting. We can also use them in workbook to view specific metrics.

The most important part is to practice, please set aside a time to practice the queries on a regular basis.

Remember, a query can be written a various way and as pre-written query can be rewritten with some improvements.

And within this book, have covered one of the simplistic ways to learn and adopt KQL while using Microsoft Sentinel, you can always expand more with references provided.

Within this book, our focus will primarily be on leveraging KQL for Microsoft Sentinel. We will embark on a journey that begins with a foundational understanding of how to construct our first KQL query.

The book is structured as follows:

Quick Start: Start our KQL journey swiftly and obtain quick results.

Filtering for Better Results: Learn techniques for filtering data to refine and improve query results.

Leveraging Joins: Explore the power of joins in KQL to combine data from multiple sources and enrich our analysis.

Summarize for Perspective: Discover the art of summarizing data to gain a broader perspective and derive meaningful insights.

Saving and Reusing Queries: Master the practice of saving and reusing queries for enhanced productivity and efficiency.

Applying Visualizations: Uncover the potential of visualizations in KQL to present data in a clear and compelling manner.

Building Use Cases: Explore practical use cases where KQL can be applied effectively in the context of Microsoft Sentinel.

Throughout the book, a step-by-step guidance is provided for real-world examples and best practices to ensure a comprehensive understanding of KQL within the Microsoft Sentinel environment.

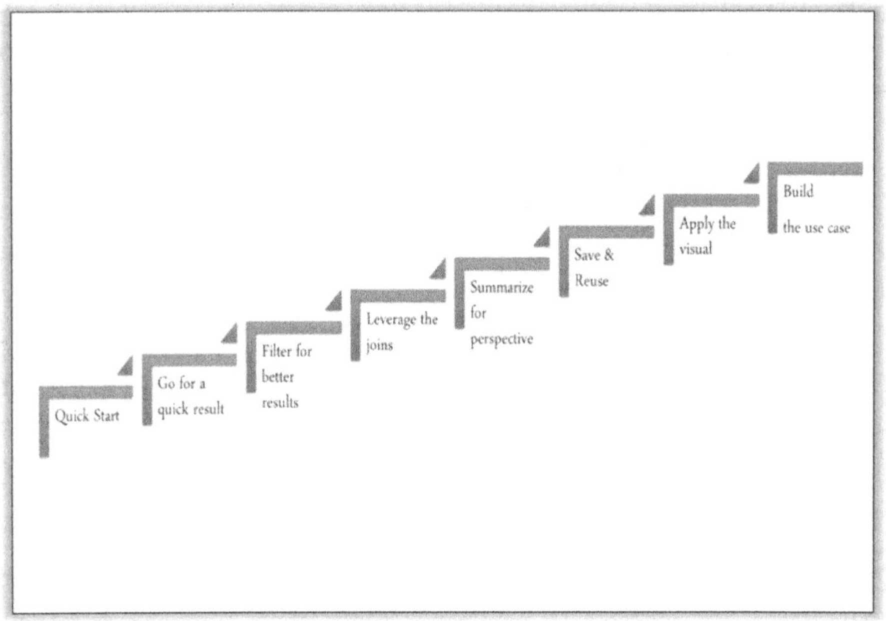

And further we will do a deep dive of each of the sections for ease of understanding and application.

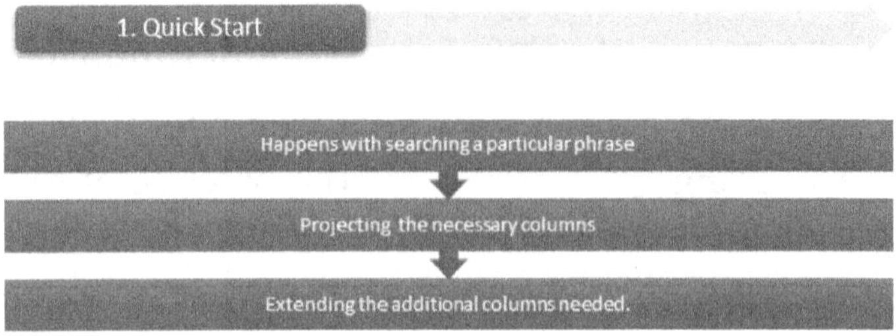

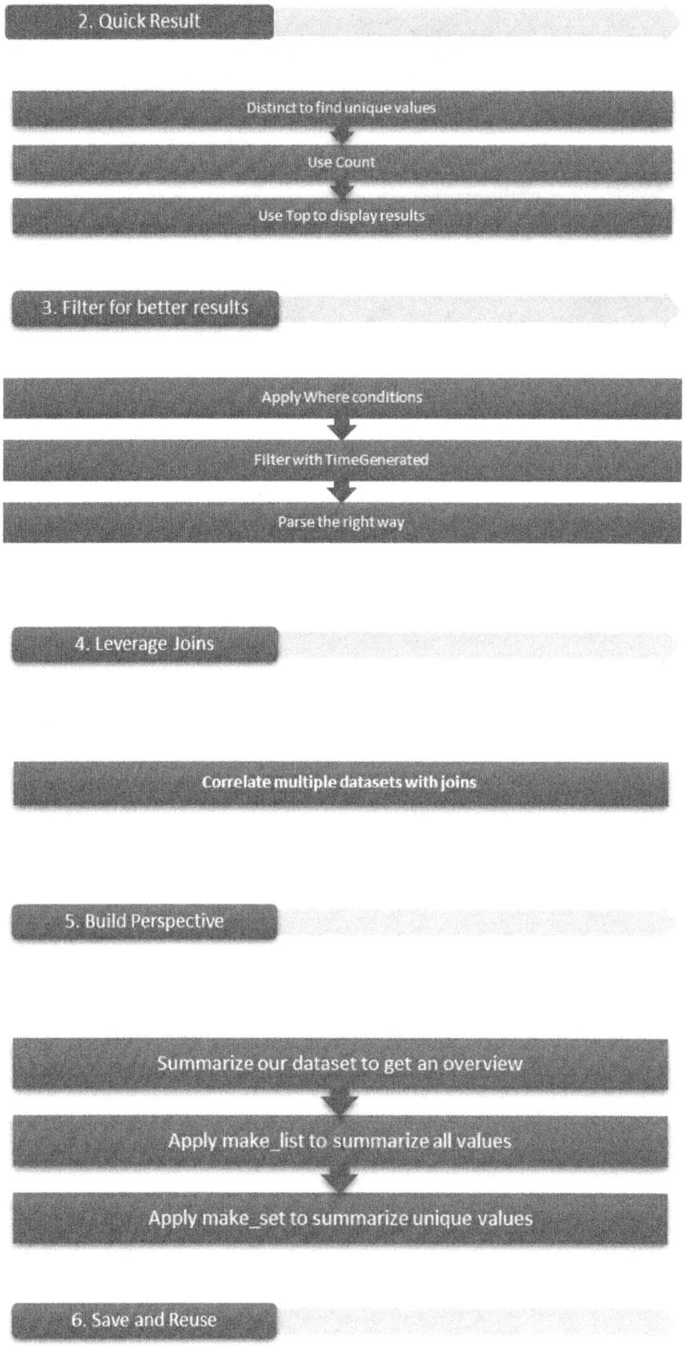
2. Quick Result
Distinct to find unique values
Use Count
Use Top to display results
3. Filter for better results
Apply Where conditions
Filter with TimeGenerated
Parse the right way
4. Leverage Joins
Correlate multiple datasets with joins
5. Build Perspective
Summarize our dataset to get an overview
Apply make_list to summarize all values
Apply make_set to summarize unique values
6. Save and Reuse

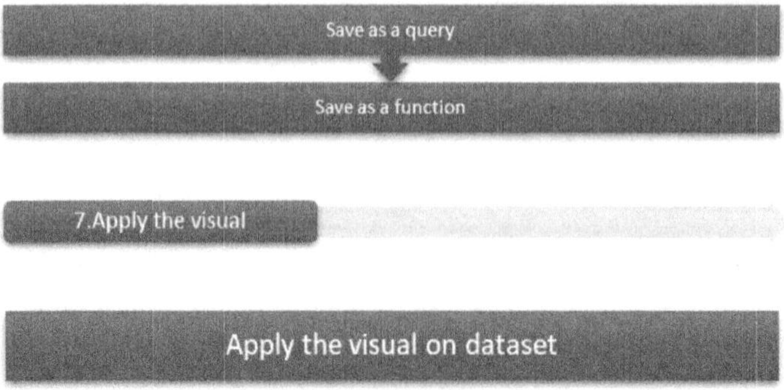
Save as a query
Save as a function
7.Apply the visual
Apply the visual on dataset

◆ ◆ ◆

KNOW & BREAK THE LIMITS

As we conclude our exploration of KQL with Microsoft Sentinel, we now turn our attention to the notion of breaking limits and pushing boundaries in security analysis. Throughout this book, we have learnt the essential knowledge and skills in KQL, enabling us to perform powerful data analysis and gain valuable insights. In this chapter, we conduct a challenge to think beyond the conventional and encourage us to explore innovative techniques, advanced concepts and emerging trends that can elevate our security analysis capabilities to new heights.

Here are a few I have found useful though my journey...

- ✓ *The limit of the results is 30K in the KQL window. But we can always use keywords like make_set , summarize etc. to fit more in less.*
- ✓ *While using a search, try to specify the column name for a faster result.*
- ✓ *Try to use == over contains for more efficiency.*
- ✓ *Leverage the query history to refer the old queries or the test queries us have written.*
- ✓ *Use Time filter as the first filter always in the query to make the most out of query.*
- ✓ *Leverage saved function for the queries us use daily.*
- ✓ *Use take operator to take the sample of a dataset.*
- ✓ *Use sort to sort the results.*
- ✓ *Leverage the cheat sheets mentioned in the reference sections.*

And here is our space to have us own.

◆ ◆ ◆

CONCLUSION

◆◆◆

As we reach the end of this book, it is my sincere hope that you have gained valuable insights, practical skills and a newfound confidence in harnessing the power of Kusto Query Language (KQL) in Microsoft Sentinel. Throughout this journey, we have explored the depths of security analytics from the weeds of data by querying, filtering, joining, summarizing, visualizing and more. And we have also learnt how to transform raw data into meaningful insights that drive effective decision-making and enable proactive threat detection.

Throughout the journey, have emphasized the importance of continuous learning and experimentation. KQL is a versatile and dynamic language that evolves alongside the ever-changing threat landscape. As new data sources, analytics capabilities and detection techniques emerge, it is essential for security practitioners to stay up to date, explore new possibilities and adapt their query techniques accordingly.

Remember, the knowledge and skills us have acquired in this book are not just theoretical concepts, they are meant to be applied in real-world scenarios. Whether we are an experienced security professional or a budding analyst, the practical examples, use cases and best practices shared throughout this book will guide us in our quest to fortify our organization's security posture.

But the journey doesn't end here. Security analytics is an ever-evolving field and the threat landscape continues to evolve at an unprecedented pace. It is crucial to stay curious, continue learning and adapt to emerging trends and technologies. As us move forward, I encourage you to stay engaged with the vibrant community of security professionals, share experiences and contribute to the collective knowledge that drives our industry forward.

I would like to express my deepest gratitude to you, the reader for accompanying me on this exploration of KQL in Microsoft Sentinel. Your dedication to advance our security analytics skills and commitment to protecting organizations from cyber threats inspires me. I also extend my gratitude to the team at Microsoft for their continuous innovation and for providing a robust platform like Microsoft Sentinel that empowers security professionals worldwide.

As us embark on our continued journey, remember that security is a collaborative effort. Share our knowledge, mentor others and contribute to the broader mission of securing our digital world. Together, we can build resilient defenses, stay one step ahead of adversaries and safeguard what matters most.

Thank you for being a part of this incredible journey. I wish us success, fulfillment and endless discoveries as you continue to unlock the power of KQL and elevate our security analytics to new heights.

◆ ◆ ◆

REFERENCES

While I am writing this book based on my experience being with KQL and learning from my contribution towards Microsoft Sentinel, Microsoft KQL documentation has been immensely helpful during the journey.
A few more worth mentioning.

As we conclude our journey through the world of KQL and Microsoft Sentinel, it is essential to acknowledge the vast array of resources and references that have contributed to the learning experience. In this final chapter, we provide a comprehensive list of references, including books, articles, documentation, online communities and other valuable sources of information, to serve as a guide and springboard for ongoing exploration and growth in the field of security analysis and here they are:

Recommended course:
Udemy Course: https://www.udemy.com/course/learn-kql-for-microsoft-sentinel/

Recommended books:
Must Learn KQL by Rod Trent:
https://github.com/rod-trent/MustLearnKQL
https://www.amazon.com/Must-Learn-KQL-Essential-Cloud-focused/dp/B0B1B62JW2

Documentation and official references:
https://learn.microsoft.com/en-us/azure/sentinel/kusto-resources

https://learn.microsoft.com/en-us/azure/sentinel/kusto-overview
https://learn.microsoft.com/en-us/azure/data-explorer/kusto/query/sqlcheatsheet
https://learn.microsoft.com/en-us/azure/data-explorer/kusto/query/splunk-cheat-sheet

https://learn.microsoft.com/en-us/azure/data-explorer/kusto/

query/kql-quick-reference

Online communities and forums:

Microsoft Sentinel Community: https://github.com/Azure/Azure-Sentinel

KQL Search Website: https://www.kqlsearch.com/

KQL Overview by John Savill: https://www.youtube.com/watch?v=Pl8n6GaWEo0

Demo Workspace to practice: https://portal.azure.com/#blade/Microsoft_Azure_Monitoring_Logs/DemoLogsBlade

The references provided in this chapter are valuable assets for our ongoing journey in KQL and security analysis. By leveraging these resources, we can tap into the collective wisdom and experiences of experts, gain diverse perspectives and continuously expand our knowledge base. The field of cybersecurity is ever evolving and staying informed, connected and equipped with the right resources is crucial for our professional growth and effectiveness in safeguarding our organization's assets.

◆ ◆ ◆

Made in the USA
Monee, IL
04 November 2026

67379626R00079